Case Studies in Marketing: An Annotated Bibliography and Index

by
Linda & Barry Berman

The Scarecrow Press, Inc.
Metuchen, N.J.   1971

ISBN 0-8108-0403-4

Library of Congress Catalog Card Number 75-155282

As Always, to our Parents
and
Grandparents

Table of Contents

Acknowledgments

The authors would like to thank Dr. Theodore C. Hines of Columbia University School of Library Service for his inspiration, assistance and encouragement.

Introduction

This book is intended primarily for instructors of marketing and related subjects (both on undergraduate and graduate levels), marketing managers and industrial training staffs. The authors have long recognized the usefulness of case study material in helping students to conceptualize ideas, in assisting marketing managers to see their company problems in proper perspective, and in training both of these groups to use analytical tools and techniques in marketing. The major function of this book, therefore, is to aid the user in selecting relevant case studies for his particular need.

Approximately 1400 case studies from 28 texts in marketing have been indexed and annotated, making available to the user a variety of material in one volume. After the reader has made his choice based on the annotations, he can then refer to the source of the case and obtain the case study in its entirety.

Scope

The case studies in these 28 sources differ in length, complexity and structure. To achieve greater consistency in coverage, the authors have decided to include only those case studies which meet the following criteria: information within the case study is self-contained; minimum length is 400 words; a situation or strategy is to be evaluated and problems are to be solved; and questions are asked--either implicitly or explicitly.

The case studies included deal only with aspects of American marketing. Hence, those concerned with international marketing have been excluded.

The sources of the case studies listed here should be found easily in libraries of colleges and universities offering courses in business. All sources were published between 1958 and 1970. While most of the sources are general marketing texts, several are concerned only with retailing and marketing research. The criteria for selecting the sources were based upon their date of publication and their general availability. No attempt has been made to evaluate the sources or the case studies.

Bibliography

The book is divided in two sections: the classified bibliography of case studies and the subject index. The case studies in the bibliography are listed alphabetically by title within the chapters. The chapters, also arranged alphabetically, are fifteen broad areas within marketing, i. e. , consumer behavior, distribution, marketing research, etc.

Citations of the case studies consist of title of case, author of text, statement of illustration, and pagination. Following the citation is a brief annotation of the case. The symbol appearing to the left of each case citation is the case number, unique for each case study. It serves to aid the reader in locating a specific case when using the index.

Example of entry:

C/P19   Pan American Coffee Bureau. Hansen. il.,
diag. 142-52.
Consumer research is utilized in studying how to increase coffee consumption. Consumer surveys, statistics of coffee production and markets, and advertising research are analyzed.

"C/P19" is the case number.

"C" stands for the chapter in which the case is located, which is Consumer Behavior. (See Table of Contents for the symbols for all of the chapters.)

"P" is the first letter of the title of the case.

"19" is the number assigned to the initial words of the title of the case study, and serves to implement the alphabetical arrangement within the chapter.

"Pan American Coffee Bureau" is the title of the case.

"Hansen" is the author of the source of the case which is
Hansen, Harry L. Marketing-Text, Cases and Readings. Homewood, Ill. Irwin, 1961. (Complete citations and identification of the sources can be found in the List of Sources.)

"il. , diag. " indicates that the case has pictures as well as charts and/or diagrams.

"142-52" is the pagination of the case study in the source and stands for pages 142 through 152.

Authorship Clarification

To identify a source where the same author has written two or more books, the respective date of publication will be included after the author statement in parentheses.

Example:

Pp/Aal   A & B Chemical Co. Bursk (1962). diag. 458-67.

Untitled Case

In the situation where a case study does not have a distinct title, one has been assigned from the text of the case, based on the name of the company involved, either real or fictitious. Where this is not possible, the case will be labeled "Untitled, " and listed alphabetically by "U" with the cases for the particular chapter.

Example:

D/Unt1   Untitled. Converse, Huegy and Mitchell. 647-8.

Case Duplication

When the same case study appears in two or more sources, only one entry for the case has been made, but reference to all sources is indicated.

Example:

Mo/L34   Latexet Rubber Co. Bursk (1962). il. , diag. 540-52; Bursk and Greyser. 166-77.

This case, therefore, may be found in both Bursk, Text and Cases in Marketing, pages 540 to 552, and Bursk and Greyser, Advanced Cases in Marketing Management, pages 166-177.

Subject Index

The second part of the book is the alphabetical subject index. The index details the specific problem areas in marketing illustrated by each case. In addition to the problem areas, the company name (when real) and the industry or product of each case are listed in the index. (There are no entries for the author or title of the sources.)

The symbol after the terms in the index is the case number. (See page viii for the explanation of the case number.) This represents the location of the case study by chapter and within the chapter.

Example of Index Entries:

(1)   Private brands, competition, Pp/D75, Pp/M19, R/G83, R/Su7

(2)   RCA Communications, Inc., Mp/R11

(3)   Razor blades, Marlin Firearms Co., N/M34

Entry 1- This indicates that four case studies deal with private brand competition. The first two cases are broadly concerned with Product Planning (Pp) and have the respective case numbers D75 and M19. The last two cases are in the general retailing area and may be found in the chapter on Retailing (R) by using their respective case numbers, G83 and Su7.

Entry 2- This indicates that the case study deals with a situation in a real company, RCA Communications, Inc. The general nature of the case is the company's Marketing Program (Mp) and it may be located in the chapter on Marketing Program by using the case number R11.

Entry 3- This indicates that a particular case study deals with a situation in New Product Planning in the real company, Marlin Firearms, which manufactures

razor blades. The case is in the New Product
Planning chapter (N) and may be located by using
the case number M34.

List of Abbreviations

assn.	association
co.	company
corp.	corporation
diag.	diagrams
il.	illustrations
inc.	incorporated
ltd.	limited

Symbols for the chapters, as used in the case numbers, are in parentheses to the left of the chapter headings in the Table of Contents.

List of Sources

Alexander, Ralph S., Cross, James, and Hill, Richard M.
Industrial Marketing. 3d ed. Homewood, Ill., Irwin,
1967.

Boyd, Harper W. Jr., Clewett, Richard M. and Westfall,
Ralph. Cases in Marketing Strategy. Homewood, Ill.,
Irwin, 1958.

Boyd, Harper W. Jr. and Westfall, Ralph. Marketing Re-
search--Text and Cases. Homewood, Ill., Irwin, 1964.

Brown, Milton P., England, Wilbur B. and Matthews, John
B. Jr. Problems in Marketing. 3d ed. N. Y., Mc-
Graw Hill, 1961.

Bursk, Edward C. Cases in Marketing Management. Englewood Cliffs, N. J., Prentice-Hall, 1965.

Bursk, Edward C. Text and Cases in Marketing. Englewood
Cliffs, N. J., Prentice-Hall, 1962.

Bursk, Edward C. and Greyser, Stephen A. Advanced Cases
in Marketing Management. Englewood Cliffs, N. J.,
Prentice-Hall, 1968.

Buskirk, Richard. Cases and Readings in Marketing. rev.
ed. N. Y., Holt, Rinehart and Winston, 1961.

Buskirk, Richard. Principles of Marketing: The Management View. rev. ed. N. Y., Holt, Rinehart and Winston,
1966.

Converse, Paul D., Huegy, Harvey W. and Mitchell,
Robert V. Elements of Marketing. 7th ed. Englewood
Cliffs, N. J., Prentice-Hall, 1965.

Corey, E. Raymond. Industrial Marketing: Cases and
Concepts. Englewood Cliffs, N. J., Prentice-Hall, 1962.

Engel, James F. , Wales, Hugh G. and Warshaw, Martin R. Promotional Strategy. Homewood, Ill. , Irwin, 1967.

Faville, David E. Selected Cases in Marketing Management. Englewood Cliffs, N. J. , Prentice-Hall, 1961.

Ferber, Robert, Blankertz, Donald F. and Hollander, Sidney Jr. Marketing Research. N. Y. , Ronald, 1964.

Gentry, Dwight L. and Shawyer, D. L. Fundamentals of Managerial Marketing: A First Course. N. Y. , Simmons-Boardman, 1964.

Green, Paul E. and Tull, Donald S. Research for Marketing Decisions. Englewood Cliffs, N. J. , Prentice-Hall, 1966.

Greif, Edwin C. Basic Problems in Marketing Management. Belmont, Calif. , Wadsworth, 1967.

Hansen, Harry L. Marketing-Text, Cases and Readings. Homewood, Ill. , Irwin, 1968.

Lockley, Lawrence C. and Dirksen, Charles J. Cases in Marketing. 3d ed. Boston, Mass. , Allyn and Bacon, 1964.

McCarthy, Jerome E. Basic Marketing: A Managerial Approach. Homewood, Ill. , Irwin, 1968.

McGregor, C. H. and Chakonas, Paul C. Retail Management Problems. 4th ed. Homewood, Ill. , Irwin, 1970.

Rachman, David J. and Elam, Houston G. Retail Management Cases. Englewood Cliffs, N. J. , Prentice-Hall, 1968.

Raymond, Robert S. Basic Marketing. Cleveland, World, 1967.

Rewoldt, Stewart H. , Scott, James D. and Warshaw, Martin R. Introduction to Marketing Management; Text and Cases. Homewood, Ill. , Irwin, 1969.

Stanton, William J. Fundamentals of Marketing. 2nd ed. N. Y. , McGraw-Hill, 1967.

Thompson, Donald L. and Dalrymple, Douglas J. Retail Management Cases. N. Y. , Free Press, 1969.

Weilbacher, William M.   Marketing Management Cases.
   N. Y. , Mcmillan, 1970.

Westfall, Ralph and Boyd, Harper W.   Cases in Marketing
   Management.   Homewood, Ill. , Irwin, 1961.

- PART I -
CASE BIBLIOGRAPHY AND ANNOTATIONS

C/Az8   Aztec Electronics.   Buskirk (1966).   778-9.
         An electronic manufacturer proposes to enter the
         market for automatic garage door openers.

C/B21   Ball Brothers.   Bursk (1962).   69-70.
         A successful marketing program for a product of a
         company acquired through a diversification entails a
         study of product features and consumer preferences
         to determine the most significant demand factors.

C/B38   The Beckman Shoe Store.   Gentry and Shawyer. 266-8.
         Two questionnaires designed to indicate buying be-
         havior and product image are compared.

C/B43   Bender Mattress Co. Bursk (1962). 75-8; Bursk (1965).
         8-11.
         A company, in its attempts to increase unit sales,
         mails questionnaires to determine the effect of vari-
         ous factors on purchases and to study any changes
         in its promotional mix.

C/B73   Bramton Co.   Bursk (1965).   diag. 12-3.
         A market survey using interviews is undertaken to
         determine whether a company should enter a market.
         The analysis presents the company's purchasing
         practices, inventory policy, equipment used, pric-
         ing, and distribution policy.

C/B98   Buying an Automobile.   Bursk (1962).   218-2;
         Bursk (1965). 5-6.
         A selling situation, in which a couple's attitudes
         towards buying when faced with two different sales
         methods, is discussed and evaluated.

C/C12   Caldwell.   Rachman and Elam.   diag. 29-38.
         Conclusions are drawn as to store image and store
         preferences of consumers based on analyses of
         consumer surveys.

C/C14   The Camden Products Co. Gentry and Shawyer.
244-5.
The role of the behavioral scientists in analyzing
consumer behavior is highlighted.

C/C51   Cladiron City.   Lockley and Dirksen.   70-1.
A town decides to close shops on Sunday despite
the custom of consumers to shop on Sundays.

C/C85   The Cranberry Growers Cooperative. Raymond. 71-3.
In order to promote an advertising campaign which
should stimulate product sales, a growers' cooperative engages a firm to do a market research study
to determine the image of the product and consumer
buying motives.

C/D23   The Danta Villanova Glass Corp.   Lockley and
Dirksen.   65-7.
This case studies and evaluates the use of consumer opinions which sway the company to produce
an inferior product.

C/D35   Decision at Boling Brother's Department Store.
Bursk (1962).   45-6.
The analysis of a store's brand policy in relation
to consumer brand preference is presented.

C/F22   Farmcrafter, Inc.   Bursk (1962).   diag.   71.
To determine the nature and strength of the demand
for a new product, a company mails different offers of prices for the product and tabulates the
results.

C/G34   Giant Food Stores.   Rachman and Elam.   90-5.
A decision by a food chain to discontinue issuing
trading stamps is countered by a lengthy evaluation
of the store's policies and its customers prepared
by the issuer of the trading stamps.

C/G92   Gruen Watches.   Lockley and Dirksen.   61-5.
A study done by Consumer's Research is analyzed
to determine the effect it has on the reaction of
consumers.

C/H31   Hawaiian Pineapple Co. Bursk (1962). diag. 295-8.
A market research study involving consumer

reactions to product quality is done to facilitate the
company's efforts in expanding demand for its
product.

C/H83 How Can the Data be Obtained? Ferber, Blankertz
and Hollander. 268-71.
A study is undertaken to determine the degree of
influence of individual family members on sample
surveys.

C/In2 Independent Grocers' Alliance Distributing Co.
Boyd, Clewett and Westfall. 111-6.
An organization undertakes a market survey in order
to determine its public image. It then compares the
image obtained to its intended objectives.

C/Iv9 Ivy Red. Buskirk (1961). 50-1.
The implications of introducing a new drug and
marketing it to the consumer market are studied.

C/K84 The Korn Publishing Co. Gentry and Shawyer. 94-5.
Different socio-economic classes in a market cause
the publisher to vary selling techniques and distribution channels to meet all segments.

C/L72 The Little Swamper. Buskirk (1961). 60-1.
The potential market for a newly-devised product is
analyzed.

C/M58 Midway Electronics Co. Buskirk (1961). 48-9.
In order to determine the economic feasibility of
marketing a new product, a company analyzes its
potential market and the buying motives of the potential consumers.

C/M69 Mission-Bell Co. Greif. 21-6.
Varying viewpoints on motivation research, including those of Bursk, Dichter and Martineau are
presented.

C/N31 The Negro Market. Greif. 60-3.
The significance of the Negro market, its growth,
changes, and role as a consumer group are
examined.

C/Or4 The Oriole Cigar Corp. Gentry and Shawyer. 245-6.

The nature of the product (cigars) and its traditional image necessitate modification before the product can be made to appeal to a new market.

C /P11   Pacific Plywood, Inc. Buskirk (1961). 58-9.
A newly hired sales executive of a firm investigates the potential buyers of his firm's product and the buying habits associated with the use of the product.

C /P19   Pan American Coffee Bureau. Hansen. il., diag. 142-52.
Consumer research is utilized in studying how to increase coffee consumption. Consumer surveys, statistics of coffee production and markets, and advertising research are analyzed.

C /P66   Piper Study Aids, Inc. Gentry and Shawyer. 472-4.
A survey of a potential market is made to determine characteristics and attitudes with which to forecast sales volume.

C /P95   Prune Research (A). Bursk (1962). il., diag. 79-86.
A research report studying the image held by consumers of a product is studied for its implications on effective advertising strategies.

C /P951   Prune Research (B). Bursk (1962). diag. 87-95.
In an effort to validate a previously done market study, an association does another study to determine consumer attitudes towards its product by using the method of word association. The association hopes the study reveals information on advertising copy.

C /P97   Pure Test Farms Dairy. Bursk (1962). 163-5.
In deciding to market a new product, a company undertakes a consumer survey using questionnaires to measure product acceptance, price decision, product name and promotional appeals.

C /R15   The Rand Co. Greif. 44-6.
In developing the consumer market for its product, a company examines the need to inform the consumer of the nature of the product, to understand

the motives for buying the product, and for
establishing effective sales techniques.

C /R22   Readiness to Buy Certain Consumer Goods.
Bursk (1962). diag. 313-21.
A technique to analyze effectiveness of marketing
strategies utilizes predisposition measures as
measures of the readiness-to-buy of consumers.

C /Sc5   Schmidt Packing Co. Bursk (1965). diag. 14-6.
In deciding whether to produce a product, a company analyzes consumers' buying habits for anala-
gous products.

C /Se2   The Security Bank and Trust Co. Gentry and
Shawyer. 264-6.
A choice is made between using consumer questionnaires or group interviews to study the image
of a bank.

C /Se5   Seneca Falls Chamber of Commerce. McGregor and
Chakonas. diag. 3-9.
In order to meet the needs of the shoppers in a
changing trading area, a survey of shoppers'
attitudes and needs is taken and analyzed to aid
retail merchants in the area.

C /Se51   The Senior Citizen Market. Greif. 64-6.
The role of the senior citizen market as a consumer group is discussed from the point of view
of product preferences, design, and pricing.

C /Se6   Services of the Consumer Advisory Council.
Greif. 32-4.
The role, functions and effectiveness of the Con-
sumer Advisory Council are examined.

C /Se7   Settling the Buyer's Qualms. Ferber, Blankertz
and Hollander. 586-8.
A home builder researches the uneasiness of
recent buyers concerning their purchase and attempts to alleviate their anxiety caused by the
purchase.

C /Sh1   Shaefner Co. Westfall and Boyd. 71-7.
Attempting to increase sales, a marketing vice

president develops a market research study to determine the image of the company, its products, and its competitors.

C /Sp4   The Spiegel Cruise Service. Gentry and Shawyer. 116-8.
A firm analyzes its market and buying motives for use in its marketing strategy.

C /St9   Studying Consumer Purchase Plans. Ferber, Blankertz and Hollander. 231-3.
The use of a continuous consumer panel operation to study consumer major purchase intentions is studied.

C /Su7   Sure Catch. Buskirk (1961). 52-3.
Before an item is produced on a large scale, the potential market for it is carefully scrutinized, including its sales potential and consumer buying motives.

C /V83   Vitamins, Paints, and Mowers. Greif. 28-31.
The area of consumer education and the role of Consumers Union are evaluated.

C /W15   The Walker Music Corp. Gentry and Shawyer. 115-6.
The strong role of consumer buying behavior in relation to new product line development is shown.

C /W52   Western Gypsum Co. Buskirk (1961). 54-5.
In order to market a new product, a company analyzes the buying motives of the product's potential customers, the potential market and a successful marketing strategy.

C /Y8   The Youth Market. Greif. 57-9.
The nature of the youth market, its implications as a powerful consumer group and the nature of its buying motivation are discussed.

Distribution

D /Ac6   Acme Chemical Co.   Alexander, Cross and Hill.
         diag. 551-6.
         A company studies its sales operation to deter-
         mine direct distribution costs of its products
         which were distributed through the company's
         twelve sales divisions.

D /Am3   American Motors Corp. Rewoldt, Scott and
         Warshaw.   363-8.
         Trying to strengthen its dealer organization, an
         automobile manufacturer considers granting
         franchises to dealers of competitive manufacturers
         to operate dual agencies.

D /An1   Analysis of Distribution Costs.   Bursk (1962).
         333-44.
         An analysis of costs of marketing operations
         details the techniques of distribution cost analysis
         and mathematical programming analysis.

D /An11 Anchor Hocking Glass Corp. Raymond.   120-2.
         As a result of a consumer survey indicating where
         consumers expect to find particular products, the
         company considers distributing its line to depart-
         ment stores.

D /Ap2   Apex Food Manufacturing Co. Greif. 193-5.
         A food manufacturer investigates more efficient
         ways of physically distributing its products.   Pool
         cars and public warehouse inventories are methods
         suggested.

D /B19   Baldwin Supermarket.   Boyd, Clewett and West-
         fall.   85-6.
         A supermarket owner must decide whether to ac-
         cept different product lines which might change the
         store image.

D /B27   The Barry Corp.   Alexander, Cross and Hill. 570-5.

25

A shock and vibration control equipment manufacturer decides on the distribution channels to market a new product.

D/C16   Camite Co., Inc. Lockley and Dirksen. 98-100.
         The question of using a sales agent rather than
         direct selling, as well as electronic distributors
         rather than direct dealer sales is examined.

D/C17   Capri's. Faville. 122-4.
         The obligations of a retailer taking on an exclusive
         line, and the considerations governing a manufac-
         turer when granting a store an exclusive agency,
         are analyzed.

D/C171   Carborundum Co. McCarthy. 716-9.
         A sales manager is faced with a threat from a
         competitor who changes the distribution method to
         one eliminating the customary distributor network
         and accompanying price schedules.

D/C172   The Carborundum Co. Bursk (1962). diag. 433-
         46; Bursk (1965). 51-62.
         A company, in deciding to change its distribution
         policy in an area, analyzes the market for the
         product in that area and determines what types of
         distributors would be best.

D/C19   Cargo. Buskirk (1961). 106-7.
         The choice of a distribution channel for a newly
         developed game is considered among wholesalers,
         direct mail and retail outlets.

D/C38   Charlton Antennas, Inc. Greif. 152-4.
         A company chooses among several possible means
         of distribution, being manufacturer's agents, sell-
         ing agents, and its own selling force.

D/C42   The Childers Machine Co. Alexander, Cross and
         Hill. 575-8.
         A manufacturer of industrial grinders must select
         a new distribution channel for the Boston area.

D/C43   Chickering Co. Brown, England and Matthews.
         diag. 315-21.
         In an effort to increase its sales volume, a com-
         pany plans to distribute its product through supply
         houses and wholesalers.

D/C67   Column Records, Inc. Raymond. 175-7.

A record company proposes to establish a branch office in place of an independent distributor.

D /C72   Columbus Steel Co.   Boyd, Clewett and Westfall. diag.   120-3.
In marketing a relatively new product, a company tries several distribution channels and sales methods.

D /C81   Carson Products Co.   Hansen.   450-4.
The merits of using a mill supply distributor or a machinery manufacturer as suppliers are studied.

D /C84   The Craft Chocolate Co.   Greif.   197-9.
A company's loading and unloading procedure highlights factors in materials handling processes and equipment.

D /C86   Crescent Wholesale Co.   Converse, Huegy and Mitchell.   642-4.
The formation of a voluntary group of retailers by a service hardware wholesaler is discussed with regard to policies and management.

D /C861   Crevier, O'Shea Co.   Brown, England and Matthews.   258-66.
An extensive description of a food brokerage organization and policy is followed by an analysis of new account selection.

D /C87   Crockett Electric Co.   Stanton.   391-2.
A company decides whether its new product is a consumer or industrial product and what distribution channels to select for the type of market.

D /D48   Determination of the Marketing Mix.   Lockley and Dirksen.   263-6.
A brief summary of several companies is given, highlighting their respective distribution policies.

D /D54   The Diamond Co.   Faville.   diag.   102-5.
A farming implement development company studies the alternative channels of distribution for its new combine.   Pricing and promotional policies are discussed.

D /D69   Doll House Products, Inc.   Westfall and Boyd.
diag.   200-6.
In trying to reach new markets, a company dis-
tributes its products to retail outlets.   In that
this policy meets with complaints from agents and
jobbers, a complete appraisal of the distribution
policy is made.

D /Ed3   Edgewood Knitting Mills.   Faville.   111-2.
A company must reformulate its qualifications for
manufacturer's agents in selecting and locating in
new geographical market areas.

D /El6   The Elmstown Manufacturing Co.   Boyd, Clewett
and Westfall.   77-80.
In reviewing the sales of its line, a company
decides to review distribution policies and evaluate
the merits of its salesmen, manufacturer's agents
and wholesalers.

D /F11   Fab-Bilt Homes, Inc.   Hansen.   diag.   454-62.
A program designed to sell a company's potential
output of prefabricated houses is outlined with
respect to outlets, real estate dealers, contractors,
builders and department stores.

D /F26   Fashion-Line Luggage Co.   Stanton.   392-4.
In order to increase a company's sales volume,
a change is made from a selective distribution
policy to one that is intensive.

D /F48   Film Life.   Buskirk (1961).   123-4.
The problems in distributing a product to a company which uses its own name for the product are
examined.

D /F95   Fuget Co.   Converse, Huegy and Mitchell.   diag.
636-8.
The decision to move into a new warehouse raises
questions of savings accrued by necessary reorganization of the office work.

D /G16   The Gardinier Co.   Greif.   165-7.
The use of manufacturer's agents in lieu of a
company sales force is studied.

D /G28   General Home Products Co. Raymond. 195-6.
A soap product manufacturer analyzes the need for
limited function wholesalers as a substitute for a
sales force.

D /G285   General Mills. Hansen. 481-3.
The analysis of a distributor and dealer organization involving marketing through independent distributors and retailers is made.

D /G55   Goetz Co. Boyd, Clewett and Westfall. 21-3.
A company analyzes its market to determine
whether it should accept a manufacturer's offer
to buy the company.

D /G65   The Gordon Chemical Co. Gentry and Shawyer.
136-8.
In order to have its new product reach retail outlets, a company investigates the use of wholesale
merchants, brokers, and company sales force.

D /G75   Grace Fabri-Tool Co. Boyd, Clewett and Westfall. 124-8.
A company, manufacturing expensive tools, tries
to adopt a distribution policy that will sell and
service the product.

D /G83   Greenfield Co. Faville. 139-42.
A company manufacturing household products revises its distribution policies to increase the number of retail outlets and the sales volume of its
products.

D /G831   Greenfield Distributors, Inc. Thompson and Dalrymple. diag. 253-67.
An analysis of the operations and management of
a wholesale food distributor is undertaken to make
improvements in present operating conditions.

D /G89   Grocery Specialties, Inc. Westfall and Boyd. diag.
488-91.
A company's desire to enter the Eastern market
has implications upon establishing a sound physical
distribution method. It must use air freight and
warehouses in the East, or ship from the factory
to the market.

D/H24   Harry Glencoe Inc. Boyd, Clewett and Westfall. 128-9.
         A manufacturer's agent of only one company wishes to represent another company so as to prevent loss if one should adopt direct selling methods.

D/H29   Hausman and Wickware. Converse, Huegy and Mitchell. 673-4.
         A wholesaler tries to revitalize its operations by investigating the feasibility of a one-story warehouse.

D/H33   Hazzard Sales Co. Hansen. 196-200.
         A decision of a firm of manufacturer's representatives to obtain a franchise for new products is studied on the basis of the sales of the company and the potential of the new product.

D/H34   The Health Aid Manufacturing Co. Lockley and Dirksen. 114-7.
         A variety of possible distribution policies for a manufacturer are presented and studied.

D/H52   Hi-Gloss Polish Co. Faville. 132-6.
         A decision to expand a product's distribution channel, involving benefits and disadvantages to the sales of the product and alterations of former distribution policies, is analyzed.

D/H521   Hickey-Freeman Co. Brown, England and Matthews. diag. 299-309.
         A company's policy to foster sound dealer relations by strictly enforcing its exclusive dealership policy comes into question when branch stores, already carrying the product, locate in an area where a store has already been granted an exclusive dealership.

D/H67   Hoffman Carpet Co. Lockley and Dirksen. 80-3.
         A company's examination of its distribution policy involving the use of wholesalers rather than direct distribution is studied.

D/H71   Holden Co. Bursk (1962). diag. 397-402; Bursk (1965). 45-9.

For the purposes of determining the approximate status of trade inventories for production planning, a company decides whether to subscribe to the Nielsen Service or to devise its own wholesale inventory audit.

D /H72   The Hollywood Products Co. Greif. diag. 160-2.
Distribution channels for a new product line are chosen on the basis of research in test markets.

D /Im7   Imperial Soap Co.   Boyd, Clewett and Westfall.
diag. 100-3.
In producing a new product, a company decides on the most likely distribution channel--food brokers or direct salesmen.

D /In8   International Harvester Farm Equipment Division.
Westfall and Boyd. diag. 190-5.
Because of the increased importance of tractors, a company evaluates its distribution channels, being farm equipment dealers, selected equipment dealers, and company-owned stores.

D /In81   International Harvester Motor Truck Division.
Westfall and Boyd. il., diag. 214-21.
In trying to increase its sales, a company considers establishing additional branches even though this would entail a large capital investment.

D /Ir4   Iris Beverage Co.   Faville. 136-9.
A company, realizing a loss in profits, proposes changing its distribution policy from using its own sales force to one using food brokers and distributors.

D /J36   Jeffery Chemical Corp.   Corey. diag. 433-45.
A manufacturer encounters the problem of competing with customers as he further diversifies his output.

D /J57   Joblin Computer Machines, Inc. Greif. 181-3.
Means of distributing computer services so as to obtain market leadership are explored.

D /J95   June Mallory, Inc. Westfall and Boyd. 491-2.
The use of air freight as a method of physical

distribution is examined.

D/K12   Kaiser Aluminum and Chemical Sales, Inc.   Corey.
il. 73-80.
The dominant channel used by Kaiser to distribute
roofing sheet material has been faced with increased competition from another channel member.
Kaiser evaluates several strategies to increase its
own market share.

D/K64   Kitchens of Sara Lee.   Westfall and Boyd.   195-
200.
To reach national markets not only does a company have to determine the best method of distribution, but also must produce its perishable
line to be able to be transported.

D/K67   Klein Wholesale Drug Co.   Hansen.   200-4.
A drug wholesaler is faced with increasing competition from another wholesale company. The
solutions involve changing means of distribution or
increasing competitive promotion.

D/K74   Knickerbocker Co.   Faville.   115-6.
The establishment of a door-to-door selling
organization is discussed.

D/L22   The Lancaster Machinery Co.   Gentry and
Shawyer.   154-5.
The evaluation of the performance of one of a
company's manufacturer's agents by means of
sales statistics is made.

D/L31   Lapham Tea Corp.   Boyd, Clewett and Westfall.
86-91.
A supermarket board confers on whether or not
to stock new products. An analysis of what products to take on as well as of the procedures in
accepting new products is required.

D/L49   Led Ballast Co.   Buskirk (1961).   112-3.
A distribution channel is chosen among a manufacturer, a sales agent, a sales force, or a dealer.

D/L61   Lido Co.   Faville.   148-9.
The problems of a company's attempt to bypass

a distributor and purchase directly from the manufacturer are analyzed.

D/L81   Lockpin Hardware Co.   Converse, Huegy and Mitchell.   diag.   650-4.
A hardware wholesaler establishes a voluntary cooperative group of hardware retailers.   Problems in doing so involve the amount of savings of members and the future management of the cooperative.

D/M19   McKesson and Robbins, Inc.   Buskirk (1966).   801.
A drug wholesaler considers entering into the pharmacy business through a unique form of enterprise.

D/M29   Mal Mills Co.   Greif.   143-5.
A company studies possible distribution policies for its new product line.   Suggestions are selective or intensive distribution.

D/M33   Marengo Tobacco Co.   Faville.   108-9.
A company's decision to market its new, higher-priced goods on an exclusive basis is debated by retailers not receiving the goods.

D/M36   The Martin Orchards.   Buskirk (1961).   119-20.
The difficulty in finding a fair distributor for peaches, insuring a good price, is complicated by the perishability of the product.

D/M361   Martinson Co.   Hansen 439-44.
A number of distribution policies, including one using sales representatives, are analyzed with respect to a product.

D/M37   C.H. Masland and Sons.   Brown, England and Matthews.   diag.   244-57.
Deciding to sell its product with its sales force, and to terminate use of a sales agent, a company investigates the industry-wide distribution policies and the structure of the industry.

D/M45   The Maytag Co.   Westfall and Boyd. diag.   481-8.
A physical distribution system involving branch warehouses, primary dealer warehouses, distributor

34

warehouses, and city distributor warehouses is examined.

D /M46   The Meadows Co. Alexander, Cross and Hill. 642-8.
A manufacturer reevaluates its present distribution policy regarding large customers.

D /M58   Midway Electronics Co. Buskirk (1961). 115-6.
The establishment of company-run installation centers as distribution channels, instead of traditional auto-radio centers, is analyzed.

D /M581   Midwest Electronics Corp. Lockley and Dirksen. 127-31.
A decision to distribute a specialty product through department stores, mail order houses, manufacturer's agents, or sales agents must be made.

D /M582   Midwest Engineering Corp. Stanton. 394-6.
To maintain its high sales volume and competitive position, a company studies changing its distribution policy from one using manufacturer's agents to one using a direct sales force.

D /M583   Milano Macaroni Co. Brown, England and Matthews. diag. 267-85.
An extensive analysis of a company's marketing policy forms a backdrop to its decision to market its product to supermarkets and chain stores.

D /M66   Mine Supply Manufacturing Co. Brown, England and Matthews. 39.
Being unable to obtain adequate dealer representation for its newly developed product, a company uses its sales force as the means of distribution.

D /M662   Minute Maid Corp. Hansen. diag. 445-50.
The company's distribution policy change to direct distribution to the retailer is analyzed with regard to product prices and industry-wide distribution policies.

D /M86   Mountain Electronics, Inc. Buskirk (1961). 110-1.

The selection of distribution channels for a new product are chosen on the basis of the potential market and means of placing the product on the market.

D /N21   National Biscuit Co.   Brown, England and Matthews. 36-8.
Not being able to market a product on a direct level to retailers, the company investigates the possibility of using wholesalers as a distribution method, which would serve to decrease distribution costs.

D /N42   New Orleans Jazz Preservation Recordings, Inc. Weilbacher. 266-80.
Alternative distribution channels for a specialized new record company are analyzed.

D /N78   Normandy Cosmetics Co.   Faville. 124-7.
The question of selling a fair-traded product to a new dealer in an area already served by a franchised dealer is discussed.

D /N82   The Norton Manufacturing Co.   Gentry and Shawyer. 176-8.
The offer of a buying syndicate to a manufacturer of large appliances is discussed with regard to prices and effect on present dealer organization of the company.

D /Ob6   O'Brien's of California, Inc.   Lockley and Dirksen. diag. 281-7.
The decision of a company to distribute its product on a national level is studied based on previous distribution policies, packaging methods, sales operations, manufacturing operations, advertising and profits.

D /O19   Olympic Watch Co.   Boyd, Clewett and Westfall. 80-2.
In an effort to increase its dealer's selling ability, a company decides to develop a training program for retail sales personnel.

D /P18   The Palmer Co.   Lockley and Dirksen. 107-9.

A company policy of distribution utilizing distributors selling to a selected list of jobbers is analyzed.

D/P21   Paris by Mail Order. Hansen. 437-9.
Distribution policies are analyzed for a small perfume manufacturer with regard to mail order or large retail distribution.

D/P38   The Pennington Press. Buskirk (1961). 117-8.
The idea of distributing a hard cover novel through drugstores and supermarkets is studied.

D/P39   The Pebble Co. Boyd, Clewett and Westfall. 97-100.
A company, dissatisfied with the present sales obtained by distributors, develops an experimental sales force using door-to-door methods.

D/P81   Popular Records Co. Greif. 190-2.
The use of air freight as a means of physical distribution is debated.

D/R11   The Rack Jobber: Service to a Retailer and a Manufacturer. Greif. 156-8.
The use of a rack jobber in supermarkets is studied.

D/R24   Red Feather Oil Co. Stanton. 396-8.
Efforts are made to improve the performance of a sales district and the relationship between dealers and manufacturers.

D/R26   Regulus Clock Co. Brown, England and Matthews. diag. 61-78.
The entire marketing organization of a company is analyzed, with emphasis on its distribution policies. The company tries to increase the effectiveness of the distribution policies and lower marketing costs.

D/R28   Remote Controls, Inc. Buskirk (1966). 801-3.
A manufacturer considers reestablishing trade relations with his past distributor.

D/R52   Riverton Co. Brown, England and Matthews.

diag. 322-37.
In changing a company's system for order and delivery of its products, a new distributor-products division undertakes new physical distribution methods.

D/R66   The Roman Pharmaceutical Co.   Gentry and Shawyer. 152-4.
The use of a food broker to reach food retailers is discussed.

D/Sa3   Salem Co.   Lockley and Dirksen.   112-4.
A large retail store decides to initiate mail order selling.

D/Sa5   San Francisco Wholesale Produce Market. Faville. 127-32.
The questions involved in relocating a long-established wholesale produce market are discussed.

D/Sa8   Saunders Repair and Equipment Shop. Greif. diag. 173-6.
A study of the market reveals information on the most effective distribution channel for an automobile replacement parts manufacturer.

D/Se1   Seager Brothers. Hansen. diag. 178-89.
The merger of two food distribution wholesalers is studied in light of operating costs, activities, profitability of the merger, and voluntary groups.

D/Se11   Seaton Radio Co.   Boyd, Clewett and Westfall. 33-5.
A small car radio manufacturer investigates possible channels of distribution for his manually-produced radio.

D/Se7   Seth Johnson. Greif. 10-2.
Several means of distributing a home-produced food specialty are discussed.

D/Sp9   Springfield Machine Toolmakers, Inc. Greif. 177-9.
A distribution policy involving dual distribution is analyzed.

D /St2   Standard Oil of Indiana. Buskirk (1961). 121-2.
            The trend towards fewer super gasoline stations
            as opposed to several small stations is analyzed
            as a more effective means of marketing gasoline.

D /St4   Stetson Shirt Co. Greif. diag. 147-50.
            Analysis of automatic selling through vending
            machines is studied.

D /Su8   O. A. Sutton Corp. Hansen. il., diag. 483-90.
            An analysis of an exclusive distribution policy
            designed to secure national sales for a product
            is made.

D /T11   The Tabor Electrical Co. Lockley and Dirksen.
            87-90.
            The merits of a distribution policy using either
            company skilled engineers as the sales force or
            manufacturer's agents outside of the company are
            analyzed.

D /T22   Tecoma, Inc. Faville. 98-101.
            In developing a new product line, a company must
            establish a new distribution policy.

D /T41   Thro-Way Collar Co. Greif. 139-41.
            Reestablishing the market for a product formerly
            popular raises the question of selecting the most
            appropriate distribution channel.

D /T66   Town and Country Homes. Westfall and Boyd.
            diag. 235-42.
            An unusually high dealer turnover is studied
            along with a company's marketing program.

D /T661   Toyon Furniture Co. Faville. 112-5.
            A company reviews its policies with regard to
            using manufacturer's agents in lieu of direct
            sales force. A loss in market share brings about
            this analysis.

D /T81   Tudor Co. Faville. 150-4.
            The analysis of a company's decision of whether
            to sell to cooperative grocery wholesalers or
            direct to retailers is presented.

D /Unt1 Untitled. Converse, Huegy and Mitchell. 647-8.
The operations of different hardware wholesalers
are compared on the bases of costs and physical
distribution systems.

D /Up4 The Upjohn Co. Rewoldt, Scott and Warshaw.
diag. 353-8.
Several possible alternative marketing strategies
for new products emphasizing distribution and
sales policies are suggested.

D /V28 Van Eden Solvents Co. Lockley and Dirksen.
117-9.
In developing a new product line, a company decides on additional channels of distribution.

D /V33 Van Norden and Co. Westfall and Boyd. diag.
221-9.
A reorganization of a company by decentralization
and a change in distribution policies from branches
to independent wholesalers is studied.

D /V34 Van Paul Fashions, Inc. Lockley and Dirksen.
105-7.
The question of whether a company should maintain its present distribution policy using a sales
agent, or employ direct mail selling is raised.

D /V83 Vita-Tex Juice, Inc. Gentry and Shawyer. 495-7.
The problems of organizing physical distribution
involve questions of L.C.L. and C.L. shipments,
company trucks or contract carriers, and warehous-
ing.

D /W17 The Walter Craig Wholesale Co. Gentry and
Shawyer. 139-40.
The application of economic order quantity formu-
lae to wholesale buying is discussed.

D /W23 The Warfield Parts Co., Inc. Gentry and Shawyer.
196-7.
In an effort to evade an accusation by the Federal
Trade Commission of price discrimination due to
the use of two types of wholesale middlemen, a
company examines the feasibility of integrating to
assume the wholesaling function itself.

D /W25   The Warren Machine Tool Co. (A).   Corey.   il.,
          diag. 344-59.
          A manufacturer appraises the relative effectiveness
          of its distribution channels.

D /W251   Warren Machine Tool Co. (B). Corey.   il. 360-6.
          The impact of a merger of the product manufac-
          turer on distributors is analyzed.

D /W29   Waterbyrd Boat Co. (A). Boyd, Clewett and
          Westfall. diag. 116-20.
          The dealer and distribution policies of a company
          are studied.

D /W291   The Waterbyrd Boat Co. (B). Westfall and Boyd.
          diag. 493-8.
          The question of a company's achieving a national
          distribution is based upon its establishing new
          branch plants.

D /W48   Wentworth Clothing Co.   Boyd, Clewett and West-
          fall. 83-5.
          A company decides whether to grant a profitable
          franchise even though in doing so the image of its
          product might decline.

D /W52   Western Gypsum Co.   Buskirk (1961).   108-9.
          The idea of selling the product directly to large
          contractors and circumventing lumber yards is
          examined.

L /W57   The Whigmore Turkey Ranch.   Lockley and Dirk-
          sen. 109-12.
          The decision of a poultry farmer to can turkey
          products and market them through food brokers is
          discussed.

D /W58   White Appliance Corp.   Boyd, Clewett and West-
          fall. 106-8.
          To increase its share of the market, a company
          decides whether it should distribute its product to
          another segment.

D /W59   Whiting Corp.   Bursk (1962).   il. 324-9;   Bursk
          (1965).   40-5.
          A company redesigns its distribution policy,

entailing a strong distributor organization, a new discount schedule, training the distributor's sales force and a direct mail campaign.

D/W61   Whitney and Sons.   Faville.   142-4.
A company traditionally selling its goods by traveling salesmen proposes changing its distribution channels.

D/W68   Willow Co.   Faville.. 109-11.
A kitchenware manufacturer decides whether to distribute its products through a rack jobber.

D/W71   The Wilson Canning Co.   Gentry and Shawyer. 194-5.
A company striving for vertical integration decides whether to abandon food brokers and use its own sales force.

D/Y2   Yard Man (1958-62).   Rewoldt, Scott and Warshaw. 369-74.
A marketing program emphasizing independent distribution policies is developed over four years to offset loss of a major private brand account.

D/Y7   Yomans Paint Co.   Westfall and Boyd.   206-10.
Planning to enter the retail paint market, a company establishes its distribution policy, advertising strategies, and pricing scales.

I /C76 Continental Gypsum Co. Stanton. diag. 160-1.
A company studies the market for an industrial
product and the implications of the study on its
marketing efforts in entering an industry of a
nondifferentiated product.

I /D14 Dairymen's League Cooperative Assn., Inc.
Hansen. 385-92.
The analysis of the marketing strategy of a
machinery manufacturer supplying equipment to a
dairy product distributor is studied.

I /L49 "Led" Ballast. Buskirk (1961). 56-7.
In order to decide whether to sell his patent or
market the product himself, a man analyzes the
size of the product's market and the product's
acceptance.

I /M75 Monsanto Chemical Co. Converse, Huegy and
Mitchell. 677-8.
The decision to leave the consumer market and
remain with industrial goods is analyzed from the
point of view of promotion costs and competition
with the company's suppliers.

I /M91 The Multi-Products Tool Co. Lockley and
Dirksen. 122-5.
A company is faced with the problem of educating
the market to a new and advantageous product.

I /Sa4 Sampson Machinery Co. Lockley and Dirksen
120-2.
A manufacturer of technical products decides
on the best means of distribution to dealers
and original equipment manufacturers.

I /St8 The Strong Co. Lockley and Dirksen. 216-20.
The role of product design is seen as a strong
factor in the appeal for a product and in affecting competitive market shares.

I/Su7   Sure-Plow Co.   Lockley and Dirksen.   131-4.
         A manufacturer, distributing its product through
         wholesalers, tries to eliminate the wholesaler and
         sell directly to retail outlets.

I/T13   Tailorboard Corp.   Boyd, Clewett and Westfall.
         37-42.
         A manufacturer successfully develops a market for
         its product and plans advertising and sales policies.

L /An4   Anheuser-Busch, Inc.   Brown, England and Mat-
         thews.   diag.   637-43.
         Transcripts of hearings investigating the discrimina-
         tory pricing practices which were injurious to com-
         petitors are analyzed.

L /Ar2   Arden Farms Co.   Boyd, Clewett and Westfall.
         diag.   203-4.
         A case concerning possible price discrimination
         and monopoly practices is examined.

L /B38   The Beauty Products Manufacturing Co.   Lockley
         and Dirksen.   157-9.
         A company is faced with maintaining its present
         high price levels or lowering them.   The latter
         would involve eliminating some promotional efforts
         and thereby destroying part of the company's
         image.

L /B48   Big Value.   Rachman and Elam.   diag.   4-6.
         The implications of a discount department store
         merger bring about legal questionning by the
         Federal Trade Commission.

L /B63   The Borax Combination.   Lockley and Dirksen.
         309-12.
         A situation in which one company conspires to
         establish a monopolistic position through a combina-
         tion is evaluated.

L /C12   California Fair Trade Act.   Hansen.   817-9.
         The California Fair Trade Act, binding nonsigners
         of a resale price maintenance contract to observe
         the contract, is discussed.

L /C56   Classe Specialty Co.   Lockley and Dirksen.   301-4.
         A manufacturer's discriminatory pricing policy is
         studied and analyzed with respect to the Robinson-
         Patman Act.

L /C75   Condoly's Supermarket, Inc. Greif. 320-2.
         The Federal Trade Commission's cease and desist
         order, as legislated in the Robinson-Patman Act,
         is illustrated, involving discriminatory pricing
         and regulation of quantity discounts.

L /C76   The Consumer Protective Guild. Lockley and
         Dirksen. 308-9.
         A group of retailers band together to prevent
         false advertising claims which seem to indicate
         low prices.

L /C78   Cooperative Advertising. Greif. 315-9.
         Cooperative advertising is discussed with regard
         to its effectiveness and to the Federal Trade Com-
         mission's term "proportionately equal."

L /C81   Corvallo Drug Co. Raymond. 296-7.
         A wholesaler of drug products analyzes the effect
         of the Robinson-Patman Act on his pricing
         structure.

L /D14   Dairies, Inc. Lockley and Dirksen. 317-8.
         A case involving a claim by the Federal Trade
         Commission that a company violated antimonopolis-
         tic legislation and the subsequent refutation by the
         company is studied.

L /D38   DeLuxe Co. Lockley and Dirksen. 150-2.
         A manufacturer decides whether to accept an
         order from a retailer which would make him sell
         below cost.

L /D49   Detroit Gasoline Case. Hansen. 803-17.
         A case based on a company's violations of the
         Clayton Act as amended by the Robinson-Patman
         Act involving price discrimination is presented.

L /D67   Doe Publishing Co. Lockley and Dirksen. 297-9.
         A publisher, granting special return privileges to
         some outlets, while not to others, encounters
         legal conflicts.

L /Ed9   Edward Frank Advertising Agency. Greif. 36-8.
         A complaint by the Federal Trade Commission
         that an advertisement constituted material deception
         is analyzed.

L /Et3   Mrs. Ethel Agnew. Lockley and Dirksen. 312-4.
A case involving fraudulent sales practices and
consumer protection is presented.

L /Ex1   Excerpts from the Clayton Act. Hansen. 799-803.
Sections of the Clayton Act are analyzed.

L /F15   Fairway Sports Equipment Co. Gentry and
Shawyer. 217-9.
An order by the Federal Trade Commission that
a company label its products to make consumers
aware that they are rebuilt is discussed.

L /F31   The Federal Trade Commission and Aspirin Ad-
vertising--"Headaches for All." Bursk and
Greyser. 184-91.
A ruling of the Federal Trade Commission on
deceptive advertising practices of competing
analgesic drug manufacturers is examined.

L /H19   The Handy-Andy Appliance Manufacturing Co.
Greif. 217-9.
The decision whether to have its products fair
traded faces a company as it debates whether to
abide by resale price maintenance contracts.

L /H191   Hanover Pharmacal Co. Lockley and Dirksen.
304-8.
The decision of a drug manufacturer to adopt a
fair trade pricing policy is debated.

L /H37   The Hilmar Cosmetic Co. Lockley and Dirksen.
299-301.
A company studies its merchandising policy of
granting inducements to sales personnel in the
form of PM's and the legal aspects associated
with this policy.

L /H66   The Hodgdon Corp. Greif. 324-6.
A firm comes under attack of the Federal Trade
Commission for its practice of preticketing its
merchandise and indicating fictitious list prices.

L /J13   Jackson Lillard, Commissioner. Greif. 333-5.
Several instances in which the Federal Trade
Commission is called upon to establish rulings

with regard to price discrimination, unfair discounts, and other actions lessening competition are described.

L /J33 Jay Clay. Buskirk (1966). 788-9.
A well-known manufacturer of casual slacks and jeans refuses to sell jeans to a retailer unless he purchases other lines.

L /M25 Macy's and the War against "Fair Trade" in Liquor. Thompson and Dalrymple. 147-54.
The issue of fair trade with regard to retail liquor prices is discussed.

L /M32 Marietta Pulp and Paper Co. (A). Corey. diag. 420-8.
The problems of using reciprocity to increase sales are analyzed.

L /M321 Marietta Pulp and Paper Co. (B). Corey. diag. 429-32.
The impact of a proposed reciprocity relationship on present supplier relations, and on relations with purchasing agents is examined.

L /N21 National Resale Price Maintainance Bill. Gentry and Shawyer. 219-22.
Arguments pro and con the National Resale Price Maintenance bill are evaluated.

L /N62 The 1951 Price War in New York City. Greif. 213-5.
Arguments here concern the legal and competitive aspects of a price war among department stores resulting from the nonsigners clause of fair trade legislation.

L /P66 Pirna Oil Co. Lockley and Dirksen. 315-7.
The situation involving the legal aspects of granting exclusive contracts is studied.

L /Q2 Quality Stabilization. Greif. 328-31.
The Federal Trade Commission's ruling on price and quality stabilization is described and analyzed for implications on consumers and industry.

L /R56 Robinson-Patman Act. Brown, England and Matthews. 633-6.
The section of the act devoted to price discrimination is studied.

L /R73 Rostrizer Electric Co. Greif. 224-6.
A pricing policy utilizing fair trade agreements is debated as favoring sales to small retailers and hindering those in large chains.

L /R95 Ryan Drug Co. Hansen. diag. 819-29.
A hearing based on a company's violations in selling practices and pricing policies is analyzed.

L /S1 S and H Co. Boyd, Glewett and Westfall. 201-2.
The case involves possible violations of a state unfair sales practice act.

L /Sh2 Sherman Antitrust Act. Hansen. 495-6.
Abstracts of the provisions of the Sherman Antitrust Act are analyzed.

L /St2 Standard Brands, Inc. Boyd, Clewett and Westfall.
206.
A company's price concessions to buyers of large quantities are examined.

L /St21 Standard Motor Products, Inc. Boyd, Clewett and Westfall. 207-8.
A pricing policy of granting rebates on large quantities is considered illegal by the Federal Trade Commission.

L /T23 Telecoin Corp. Boyd, Clewett and Westfall.
202-3.
A situation involving full-line-forcing is presented.

L /T41 Three Short Cases on Marketing Legislation.
Greif. 337-40.
Decisions relating to fair trade and price fixing are described.

L /W43 J.J. Weitzel. Lockley and Dirksen. 295-7.
A retailer, establishing unfair resale·prices, comes into conflict with fair trade legislation.

Case Studies in Marketing

L /W66 Willey Electric Co. Gentry and Shawyer. 399-401.
A decision to fill an order for private label
merchandise for a corporation results in the company's receiving a cease and desist order from
the Federal Trade Commission to stop using dis-
criminatory pricing in favor of the corporation.

Marketing--General Nature

Mg/B15   Baily Co. McCarthy. 704-5.
An offer by a company to hire a sales representative to be in charge of price, advertising and sales efforts in a particular area is considered.

Mg/B22   The Banks Co. Raymond. 18-9.
The decision to open a retail furniture outlet is analyzed.

Mg/B49   Bill Byron. Buskirk (1961). 12-3.
The decision to go into a career in marketing in a small business or a large corporation is studied.

Mg/B66   Bourbon Brothers Distilling Company's Missouri Oaks Sales Decline. Weilbacher. 3-15.
A distilling company attempts to uncover the cause of a sales decline in a premium bourbon whiskey.

Mg/B96   Business: Social Responsibility and Ethics. Greif. 7-9.
The social and ethical responsibilities of business and marketing are discussed.

Mg/J33   The Jay-Sun Television Co. Greif. 3-5.
The role of marketing in relation to other activities of a company is discussed.

Mg/M46   Mead-Canton Corp. Corey. diag. 114-28.
Two market alternatives are discussed with regard to product specifications, promotion and pricing strategy.

Mg/N36   The Neshbud's Automobile Purchase. Greif. 40-2.
The relative benefits and disadvantages of financing methods such as mortgage refinancing and installment loans are examined.

Case Studies in Marketing

Mg/R33   Reynolds Products Co.   Alexander, Cross and
Hill.   diag.   653-62.
A piping product manufacturer evaluates a
location for a branch warehouse.

Mo/Aa1   AAA Plastics Co. McCarthy. 734-6.
A study of a company and the demand for its
products is made before a man decides to accept
a position as sales manager.

Mo/At8   Attracto Sales, Inc. Greif. 277-9.
Efforts of a company to raise the percentage of
profits on sales are attempted through coordinating
departmental budget plans.

Mo/Au6   Aurora Electronics Co. Stanton. 68-9.
The marketing concept is introduced to an
engineering-oriented firm which desires to expand
into non-governmental markets.

Mo/B38   Beaver Ranch Supply Co. McCarthy. 728-31.
An analysis is made of a franchised dealer's
business organization, marketing strategy, and
price discounting policies.

Mo/B54   Bissell Co. Westfall and Boyd. 363-6.
As a result of rapid expansion of a company's
product line, the firm considers reorganization
to speed new product development.

Mo/B95   Burwell Motors Division. Corey. 409-19.
An electric motor manufacturer is faced with the
problem of a rapid increase in field repair costs.

Mo/C17   Capital Food Markets. McGregor. diag. 82-6.
Formal budgeting is introduced to a food chain to
control sales and personnel costs.

Mo/C57   Clayton Co. Faville. 144-8.
Expansion in productive capacity of a company
causes it to seek a more effective distributive
organization.

Mo/C72   The Columbia Products Co. Gentry and Shawyer.

74-5.
The question of new product packaging brings to light a conflict in responsibilities of the marketing and production divisions.

Mo /D92   E.I. DuPont De Nemours and Co., Inc.   Corey. diag.   388-401.
Dupont's textile fibers department organization is analyzed with reference to its divisional structure.

Mo /F11   Factor Drive-In.   Thompson and Dalrymple.   il. 82-90.
Failure of the restaurant's owner to oversee operations results in declining employee morale and profits.

Mo /G76   The Grandholm Co.   Bursk (1962).   552;   Bursk (1965).   93-4.
The choice of a sales promotion manager is made based on his account of a promotional effort.

Mo /G94   Guilford Appliance Co.   Gentry and Shawyer. 72-4.
The marketing organization of the company is drawn to discuss the function of the marketing manager.

Mo /H11   Hadley Co.   Corey.   diag.   129-44.
The product line planning and control organization of a firm is analyzed with regard to the role of the manager.

Mo /H19   The Hancock Co. Alexander, Cross and Hill. diag. 604-10.
The role of the product development department in a chemical company is examined.

Mo /H39   The Henry Anderson Co.   Gentry and Shawyer. 40-2.
A company organizes its marketing department to sell directly to retailers instead of using manufacturer's agents.

Mo /H391 Henry Research Corp.   Westfall and Boyd.   diag. 356-63.
A company reorganizes its departments to effect better coordination between marketing and research and development.

Mo /H99   Hydraulic Systems Co.   Westfall and Boyd.   diag. 366-71.
In order for the company to expand its existing lines and enter a new market, it conducts an extensive market survey and reorganizes its marketing department accordingly.

Mo /Id2   Ideal Industries.   Westfall and Boyd.   diag. 504-9.
A sales manager develops a method for allocating sales costs to assess the product line profitability of the company's product lines.

Mo /In4   Ingram Appliance Stores.   Converse, Huegy and Mitchell.   690-1.
Due to declining profits, a company calls in a consultant who suggests changes in promotional methods, selling organization and organizational structure.

Mo /In82   International Minerals and Chemical Corp.   Westfall and Boyd.   diag.   384-9.
A possible reorganization of a company's sales force, entailing the merger of two distinct sales divisions and resulting in multiproduct sales and service, is studied.

Mo /J13   Jackson Chemical Co.   Alexander, Cross and Hill.   diag.   622-8.
The research and development group is divided into three research teams, each of which work on separate product lines.

Mo /J73   Jones Manufacturing Co.   Conversey, Huegy and Mitchell.   639-40.
The relative merits of a company's membership and activity with several trade associations are analyzed.

Mo /K98   Kyle and Evans Manufacturing Co.   McCarthy. diag.   722-7.
A construction company's main areas of business are discussed with an analysis of its objectives, marketing strategy and operations.

Mo /L34   Latexet Rubber Co.   Bursk (1962).   il.   diag. 540-52;   Bursk and Greyser.   166-77.

Decisions to hire an industrial products sales manager or a general sales manager are predicated on the overall conditions of the company.

Mo/M11   A Management Gap.   Ferber, Blankertz and Hollander.   110-5.
A consultant recommends the creation of a vice president in charge of marketing position in response to a request from the owner of a hotel complex for an analysis of his advertising program.

Mo/M31   The Manzi Brothers Supermarket.   Gentry and Shawyer.   42-4.
An analysis of a supermarket's management department is presented for recommendations for reorganization.

Mo/M34   Marks and Associates.   Boyd and Westfall.   34-6.
An advertising agency, specializing in farm and industrial accounts, decides to set up a separate marketing research department.

Mo/M58   Mid-Town.   Rachman and Elam.   diag.   39-41.
To solve a problem of declining profits relative to general industry growth, a company studies the feasibility of reorganizing its structure.

Mo/M69   Mrs. Jensen's Journal.   Thompson and Dalrymple.   57-64.
Personnel policies and organization of a department in a retail store are analyzed through a "critical incident" technique.

Mo/N 21   National Manufacturing Co.   McCarthy.   685-6.
The role of the marketing department of a new division set up to market a new product idea is changed to improve the division's performance.

Mo/N81   Northern Markets.   McGregor and Chakonas.   66-9.
The decision to establish a training program in order to fill management positions in a food chain is evaluated and ideas for a training program are studied.

Mo/O16   The Olner Co.   Westfall and Boyd.   diag.   351-6.

The multi-divisional company investigates the feasibility of forming a centralized marketing research unit.

Mo /P21   Paris House.   Rachman and Elam.   42-4.
The reorganization of the branches of a department store includes revisions of the merchandising policy.

Mo /P94   Progressive Industries, Inc.   Westfall and Boyd. diag. 344-6.
A reorganization of a company's marketing operations, involving the sales force and marketing divisions, is studied.

Mo /R34   Rheem Manufacturing Co.   Westfall and Boyd. diag. 338-44.
A company's organization plan, combatting decentralization and providing for national marketing, is studied.

Mo /Se1   Seafood Grocery Co.   Thompson and Dalrymple. 64-7.
Difficulties in the personnel structure and employee personalities of a grocery chain have caused it to to into debt.

Mo /Se4   Seifert Manufacturing Co.   McCarthy.   732-4.
An analysis of a company's marketing efforts and organization is made as a basis for evaluating its marketing strategy.

Mo /S15   Sloan and Drake.   McGregor and Chakonas.   62-5.
The organization and management of a planned branch department store are debated.

Mo /So6   Sooner Bag Co.   Buskirk (1961).   25-6.
A new business faces not only legal problems, but also financial difficulties.

Mo /Un3   Union Carbide Plastics Co.   Westfall and Boyd. diag. 347-51.
A complete reorganization of a company's marketing division is studied.

Mo /V66   Victor Advertising Agency.   Boyd and Westfall. 36-9.

The marketing research director of an advertising agency proposes a new organization for client-agency research.

Mo /W89   Worcester Co.   Hansen.   diag.   738-42.
Compensating the selling force as well as the product designers is considered by a company.

Mo /X2   Xerox.   Converse, Huegy and Mitchell.   diag. 665-6.
Aspects of sales force management, promotion and research are viewed as contributors to the company's expansion.

Mp /Ab9 A_{21}C. Buskirk (1966).   803-4.
An American firm evaluates the market and its
proposed strategy for an imported condensation
preventative.

Mp /Ad5 Adler Mattress Co.   Boyd, Clewett and Westfall.
211-3.
Attempting to boost a company's sales, the
marketing manager of a firm examines its marketing program for possible changes.

Mp /Ag3 Agex Oil Co.   Alexander, Cross and Hill.   diag.
562-9.
A refinery reevaluates its marketing operations
as they pertain to the steel industry.

Mp /Al5 Alleghany-Ludlum Steel Corp.   Corey. diag.
367-87.
A recently appointed product manager studies
how to strengthen field sales performance and
how to react to the changed effectiveness of
distribution channels.

Mp /Al8 Aluminum Co. of America.   Corey.   il. 237-47.
After continued promotion, sales of aluminum
bearings and castings failed to reach the estimated
potential.

Mp /Am3 The American Bank of Meadville.   McCarthy.
712-4.
A conservative bank is faced with competition
from a new bank with an energetic banking
policy.

Mp /Am5 AMI, Inc.   Boyd, Clewett and Westfall.   11-4.
In taking on a new product and diversifying the
product line, a company devises a completely new
market plan.

Mp/An2   Anderson and Reynolds, Inc. Lockley and Dirksen. 290-1.
In developing a new product, a company seeks to boost sales.

Mp/An8   Anthony, Inc. Hansen. diag. 876-94.
The entire company is studied with regard to developing a sound marketing plan for a product.

Mp/Ar1   Aragon Co. Faville. 323-4.
A description of a product, its decreasing sales volume, and abortive marketing attempts, highlights the need for a new marketing program.

Mp/Ar6   Arno Shoe Co. Boyd, Clewett and Westfall. diag. 223-8.
Before expanding the market of a product, a company analyzes its marketing program--its operating expenses, product line, promotion and distribution.

Mp/B11   B.T. Babbitt, Inc. Brown, England and Matthews. diag. 805-26.
In an effort to regain its market share, a company establishes a new, dynamic marketing program on a market-by-market basis.

Mp/B43   Benjamin Corp. Hansen. diag. 862-75.
A company executive decides whether to liquidate at a loss or invest in a company with a nonprofitable product.

Mp/B45   Mrs. Bernatha Cobden. Lockley and Dirksen. 38-40.
A marketing program is formulated for a handmade specialty product.

Mp/B59   Blanchard Co. Lockley and Dirksen. 125-6.
A company introducing a new product must decide on the marketing strategy, including price and distribution.

Mp/B63   Booker and Co. Buskirk (1966). 815-7.
A men's clothing manufacturer decides which alternative strategies, vertical integration or a new distribution policy, would best improve performance.

Mp/B73   Brakelator Co. Buskirk (1961). 194-5.
A marketing program for a new product, highlighting distribution channels, product name, pricing,
and selling methods, is analyzed.

Mp/B83   Brunswick-Balke-Collender Co. Boyd, Clewett
and Westfall. 228-33.
A company, diversifying its product line, must
devise a sound marketing program.

Mp/B96   The Businessmen's National Bank. Greif. 121-3.
The decision of a bank to open a new branch is
analyzed with respect to location, potential market
and promotional strategies.

Mp/C12   California Prune and Apricot Growers Assn.
Faville. 342-6.
The nature of an agricultural products cooperative
is described. Marketing agreements between the
growers and the association are studied.

Mp/C17   The Capex Co. Westfall and Boyd. 248-52.
A marketing program, concentrating on distribution methods, is developed with considerations
to price and promotion.

Mp/C64   Coccidiostats for the Birds. Alexander, Cross
and Hill. 579-81.
A chemical manufacturer finds that his drug for
chickens and turkeys is not effective in checking
disease.

Mp/C69   Collis Co. Alexander, Cross and Hill. diag.
582-9.
A paper company institutes a new system of
sales reporting and trade analysis.

Mp/C73   Comet Machinery Corp. Lockley and Dirksen.
134-7.
A company evaluates the sales of its product
lines and analyzes the sales force, price and
distribution policies.

Mp/C731 Company X. Lockley and Dirksen. 44-50.
A corporation revises its organization to adapt
to the "marketing concept" philosophy.

Case Studies in Marketing

Mp/C732 Co. "X," "Y," or "Z." Bursk (1962). 560-2.
A manufacturer must reevaluate his marketing
strategy due to a change in his market. Alternative strategies are presented for evaluation to
meet with the changed environment.

Mp/C86 A Critique of Marketing. Gentry and Shawyer.
21-2.
An overview of general practices of marketing is
given, requiring an analysis of the marketing
system.

Mp/C91 The Cundy-Belts Corp. Alexander, Cross and
Hill. 590-9.
A wholesaler, faced with increased competition,
considers whether he should change his marketing
mix.

Mp/D34 The Dean Electric Co. Boyd, Westfall and
Clewett. diag. 217-23.
In trying to establish a secure position in the
industry, a company revamps its marketing
program.

Mp/D74 Douglas Co. Hansen. diag. 894-911.
The decision-making procedure using expected
utility value to guide a company in entering a
market is studied.

Mp/D75 The Dow Chemical Co. Corey. 331-43.
A manufacturer of raw materials must reappraise
his assistance program to his fabricator customers due to changed market conditions.

Mp/D85 Ducto Co. Lockley and Dirksen. 54-6.
A company decides to concentrate on a particular
consumer market for a product and analyzes its
potential.

Mp/Ed8 Educational Electronics, Inc. Brown, England
and Matthews. il., diag. 286-98.
Having developed a new product, a company
studies the means for working out a marketing
program for it.

Mp/Ef5 Effluvia House Cosmetics Monitors its Marketing

Activities. Weilbacher. 298-320.
A control system for market planning in a department store is evaluated.

Mp /E13   Elgin National Watch Co.   Westfall and Boyd.
diag. 16-24.
A marketing plan emphasizing new product lines
and distribution plans is analyzed to deter lower
priced competitors from getting a larger market
share.

Mp /E14   Elias Instrument Co.   Brown, England and Matthews. diag. 131-52.
An extensive analysis of a company's marketing
organization and program, covering all facets of
the marketing and merchandising processes, is
studied to increase a company's sales and profits.

Mp /Ev2   The Eversharp Pen Co.   Westfall and Boyd.
diag. 530-5.
As a result of sales falling below quotas, a
company reevaluates its marketing program.

Mp /Ex6   Expansion of George Axel Co.   Converse, Huegy
and Mitchell. 668-9.
A company debates the suggestion of a consultant
to expand its operations in order to increase its
market share and meet competition.

Mp /F18   Falconbridge Nickel Mines, Ltd. Raymond. 156-7.
A firm decides what to do with excess capacity
caused by the expiration of a government contract.

Mp /G37   A.C. Gilbert Co. McCarthy. 736-8.
Efforts to meet new trends and increasing competition are made in expanding a company's product
line and promotional efforts.

Mp /G45   Glamour Vending Corp. Buskirk (1961). 27-9.
The problems of marketing a new perfume vending
service with a discussion of franchise dealerships
for such a service are presented.

Mp /G58   Golf Enterprises, Inc. Buskirk (1966). 818-9.
The marketing policy of a new gag product is
analyzed.

Mp/H36   The Heflin Chemical Supply Co. (A). Alexander, Cross and Hill. 611-5.
A well-established user of livestock feed discredits his supplier's product.

Mp/H361   The Heflin Chemical Supply Co. (B). Alexander, Cross and Hill. diag. 615-22.
A company redesigns its sales reporting system.

Mp/H46   Hesper Silver Co. Brown, England and Matthews. 827-45.
A company's decision to enter a new market involves questions of product design, brand name and distribution.

Mp/H73   Holmes Manufacturing Co. Rewoldt, Scott and Warshaw. diag. 207-13.
In deciding whether to add a new product to its existing line, a company plans its marketing program.

Mp/H75   Home Products Universal Handsome Boy Cleanser Faces a Competitive Threat. Weilbacher. 158-79.
A cleansing and home maintenance product manufacturer tests the efficiency of a new cleaning product.

Mp/H751   Home Products Universal's Distribution Policy for Handsome Boy Cleanser. Weilbacher. 321-37.
A store audit program for a cleanser is examined in terms of its ability to isolate distribution trends.

Mp/H86   Hudson Chemical Corp. Corey. diag. 248-76.
After five years of losses, a company considers whether it should accept an offer to purchase the operation.

Mp/In2   Indian Head Mills, Inc. Brown, England and Matthews. il., diag. 766-88.
In light of the failure of an advertising campaign, a company's advertising budget faces a cutback pending a review of the marketing plans.

Mp/In7   Insul-Kool. Buskirk (1966). 809-12.
The market plan for a new invention is evaluated.

Mp /J13   Jaeger Ltd. Buskirk (1966). 814-7.
An importer plans to drop a product from a line
of sweaters because of declining sales.

Mp /J31   Jason Chemical Manufacturing Works. Greif.
294-6.
A company hires a marketing manager to suggest
ways of meeting competition and of promoting its
product line.

Mp /J77   C. Joseph Instrument Co. Lockley and Dirksen.
200-3.
A company actively engaged in research and
development analyzes the question of whether to
enter into contracting agreements.

Mp /K23   The Keck Corp. Corey. il., diag. 293-313.
Problems involved with government research and
development contracts are discussed.

Mp /K67   The Kleanrite Co. Gentry and Shawyer. 58-61.
A company tries to differentiate its product from
that of its competitor.

Mp /K91   Kroehler Manufacturing Co. Westfall and Boyd.
il., diag. 49-56.
A company changes its marketing program based
on the results of a market survey.

Mp /L63   Lincoln Foundation. Lockley and Dirksen. 51-4.
The market of people of over 65 is studied in light
of its characteristics and significance for marketing.

Mp /L84   Lone Star Manufacturing Corp. Boyd, Westfall
and Clewett. diag. 42-7.
A new product developed by a company is studied
to develop a marketing program.

Mp /L96   Lub-Seal Manufacturing Co. Westfall and Boyd,
il., diag. 543-52.
Faced with a declining market share and product
use due to competition, a company plans to
develop a new sales program.

Mp /L961 Ludlow Corp. Brown, England and Matthews.
il., diag. 789-804.

The marketing program for a new product, including pricing, promotion, distribution and sales is developed.

Mp/M35 Marsh Management Consultants, Inc. Greif. 14-6. The decision of a management consulting firm to diversify its activities and obtain controlling shares in various companies is discussed from the point of view of differences in marketing functions.

Mp/M55 Merrill, Inc. (A). Rewoldt, Scott and Warshaw. 667-79.
Due to the failure of initial promotional efforts of a new product, a company has an extensive research study done to examine the market, distribution methods and sales appeal.

Mp/M551 Merrill, Inc. (B). Rewoldt, Scott and Warshaw. il., diag. 685-90.
A marketing program, involving a study of the market potential of a new product, development of new markets and an increased advertising budget, is studied.

Mp/M552 Merrill, Inc. (C). Rewoldt, Scott and Warshaw. 690-5.
A marketing program's failure is diagnosed with actions proposed to develop a profitable sales volume.

Mp/M58 Microtonics, Inc. Buskirk (1966). il. 812-4.
A company develops a marketing plan for a printed circuit quality control gauge.

Mp/M581 Mid-States Aviation Corp. Boyd, Clewett and Westfall. diag. 166-9.
A company studies its advertising, sales and costs to revise its marketing program.

Mp/M582 Mighty Mac. Buskirk (1966). 800.
A boy's outerwear manufacturer considers changing the name of its adult outerwear division.

Mp/M85 Motorola, Inc. Westfall and Boyd. il., diag. 56-61.
To boost the sales of its higher priced lines, the

company has a high quality furniture company prepare cabinets for the former's televisions.

Mp/M91 The Mullenkamp Cooperative Assn.   McCarthy.
709 707-8.
Failure of the marketing program and a decline
in demand for farm-grown tomatoes causes large
volume members of a cooperative association to
debate whether to leave the association and organ-
ize another group.

Mp/M95 Murphy Associates.   Lockley and Dirksen.   diag.
229-33.
The merger of two companies is discussed with
problems pointed out in the dealers contracts and
distribution policies.

Mp/N21 The National Washing Machine Co.   Buskirk (1966).
789-800.
A washing machine company reports losing sales
as a result of an independent testing agency's
downgrading of its product.

Mp/N42 The "New" Arnold Constable.   McCarthy. 694-5.
An attempt is made to reverse a department store's
sales decline by refurbishing the store, and
changing its promotion logo and its image.

Mp/Ow2 Owens-Corning Fiberglas Corp.   (A). Corey.
diag.   314-22.
The company encounters problems in the development of new applications for its product.

Mp/Ow21 Owens-Corning Fiberglas Corp. (B).   Corey.
323-30.
Tha manufacturer of fiberglas is faced with the
problem of how much technical service it should
provide.

Mp/P12 Packard Motor Car Co.   Brown, England and
Matthews.   diag.   202-5.
The analysis of the successes and failures of the
Packard Co., its mergers with Studebaker, and
its eventual demise, are traced.

Mp/P53 The Philip Walston Co. Gentry and Shawyer.

513-5.
In an effort to control and evaluate his company's marketing program, the president undertakes a cost analysis of the product line, the marketing operations, and past orders.

Mp/P68 Pitman-Moore Co. Buskirk (1961). 198-9.
The marketing of a drug item to be used as a food product raises problems in distribution channels, sales efforts and promotion.

Mp/P75 Pocket Books, Inc. Brown, England and Matthews. 40-3.
In producing a new product line, a company investigates the possibility of the same mass marketing techniques for the new line as for the older line.

Mp/P87 Powell and Brente. Greif. 298-300.
An idea to establish a consumer service club utilizing contractors for home-servicing is discussed from the point of view of a marketing program, capital requirements and contractor participation.

Mp/P94 Proctor, Inc. Greif. 306-8.
A company develops a marketing program geared to maintaining the company's leadership in the market and to emphasize the high quality of its product.

Mp/Q2 Quality Furniture Co. McGregor and Chakonas. diag. 244-6.
Concerned that a store is not fulfilling its potentials the management studies its market share based on estimated figures of store sales.

Mp/Q3 A Question of Marketing Costs. Gentry and Shawyer. 515-7.
Issue is taken with the definition of marketing costs as given by the U.S. Department of Agriculture.

Mp/R11 RCA Communications, Inc. Rewoldt, Scott and Warshaw. il., diag. 639-66.
A survey of potential customers sheds light on

selling and promotional plans of a service-oriented company.

Mp/R111 Robden Glass Co. Lockley and Dirksen. 40-1.
The lack of a sound market plan for the company is seen as a cause of its declining market share.

Mp/R15 "Rane-Dare" Raincoat Co. Lockley and Dirksen. 242-4.
In trying to meet competition, a company organizes a sales program involving distribution and sales force organization.

Mp/R18 The Rapids-Standard Co., Inc. Corey. il., diag. 276-95.
Problems of coordinating new product planning between field sales force and engineers are considered.

Mp/R21 Record Vending Machines, Inc. Buskirk (1961). 196-7.
A marketing program for a new invention is developed.

Mp/R27 The Reignbeaux. McCarthy. 705-7.
A retail store having a high degree of success in its marketing efforts faces competition from new shopping centers.

Mp/R38 Richards, Inc. Rewoldt, Scott and Warshaw. diag. 502-6.
The marketing efforts for introducing a new policy entail analyzing a company's sales strategy and promotional policy.

Mp/R47 The Rio Railroad. Bursk (1962). diag. 554-60; Bursk (1965). 102-8.
Faced with declining sales, a company devises a long range program with demand factors and elements of the marketing mix.

Mp/R52 Ringo. Buskirk (1966). 807.
Two business school seniors attempt to set up a marketing plan for a novelty.

Mp/Si3 The Silas Oates Co. Alexander, Cross and Hill.

diag. 663-70.
A castings company evaluates new sales opportunities.

Mp/So8   South Seas, Ltd.   Buskirk (1961).   200-1.
A marketing program is devised for the distribution
of orchids through supermarkets.

Mp/St7   L. & D. Stores, Inc.   Lockley and Dirksen.   35-7.
The marketing functions of a large retail food
chain are explained.

Mp/T17   Tartan Co.   Boyd, Clewett and Westfall.   214-7.
In introducing a new product, a sales manager
devises a marketing plan having product style, advertisements, distribution, pricing and product
appeal.

Mp/T21   The Taylor Marine Supply Co.   Alexander, Cross
and Hill.   diag.   670-5.
A privately-owned corporation has its operations
reviewed and plans future activities.

Mp/T23   Telectronics, Inc.   Rewoldt, Scott and Warshaw.
29-31.
A United States television manufacturer faces foreign competition and is forced to revise his marketing strategy.

Mp/T231 Television and the Consumer.   Lockley and Dirksen.
56-7.
The educational and recreational role of commercial
television and the role of the advertiser in deciding on the level of television broadcasts are discussed.

Mp/T36   The Thomas Electric Co.   Gentry and Shawyer.
57-8.
A marketing strategy designed to boost sales to
the civilian market is presented.

Mp/T61   Toni's Restaurant.   McCarthy.   689-90.
A marketing strategy for setting up a new business
is described with emphasis on achieving rapid
growth.

Mp/T76   Tru-Frost Division.   Boyd, Clewett and Westfall.
          223-6.
          In devising a marketing program, a company con-
          centrates on a distribution plan, pricing and pro-
          motion.

Mp/T89   TV - Stereo Sales, Inc.   Greif.   291-3.
          Several suggestions for a sales strategy are pro-
          posed, including a large field sales force and ad-
          vertising investments, or a dealer network.

Mp/Un3   Union Carbide Consumer Products Co.   Westfall
          and Boyd.   diag.   7-16.
          A comprehensive market plan is studied to offset
          increasing competition and reluctance of whole-
          salers to stock the product prior to the selling
          season.

Mp/V61   Verto-Drape Co. Faville.   diag. 312-22.
          The development of a marketing program hinging
          on maximum distribution and a low sales budget
          is studied with special regard to dealer organiza-
          tion and consumer market promotion.

Mp/W58   Whitehouse Lighting Co.   Raymond.   229-31.
          A sales manager proposes a three point program
          for increasing sales of lighting fixtures.

Mr /Ad9   To Advertise What?   Ferber, Blankertz and
           Hollander.   553-6.
           A home builder has research conducted to
           determine effectiveness of his advertising ex-
           penditures.

Mr /Am2   American Airlines.   Green and Tull.   216-9.
           The use of a questionnaire to evaluate consumer
           attitudes and user attitudes is described.

Mr /Am21   American Dairy Association.   Boyd, Clewett
           and Westfall.   diag.   23-7.
           In planning to promote a particular product, the
           association undertakes an extensive market study.

Mr /Am3   American Institute of Laundering.   Westfall and
           Boyd.   diag.   89-99.
           Faced with a rapidly changing industry, a trade
           association undertakes market research programs
           to meet industry needs.

Mr /An7   Antioch Electronics, Inc.   Faville.   56-63.
           In the process of developing a low cost product, a
           company's market research department studies its
           market potential and design and cost objectives.

Mr /Ap4   Appel Co.   Boyd and Westfall.   197-9.
           A sales manager conducts a phone survey to as-
           certain the percentage of stores stocking his com-
           pany's new products.

Mr /Ar2   The Ardmore Co.   Boyd and Westfall.   144-5.
           A toilet soap manufacturer plans to conduct re-
           search to determine what contest prizes are most
           acceptable to consumers.

Mr /Ar7   Arthur Douglas Co.   Boyd and Westfall. 236-8.
           An advertising agency develops a questionnaire to
           find out more about a prospective client's product.

Mr /At5   Atkins Coffee Co. Boyd and Westfall. 451-3.
A sales manager decides whether to accept a study of consumer container preferences performed by the advertising department.

Mr /Au6   Aurora Electronics Co. Stanton. 158-9.
Studies are done in a large city to determine the potential market for a new product.

Mr /B44   The Bentley Co. Boyd and Westfall. 562-3.
A toiletry manufacturer uses a split run test to evaluate advertising effectiveness.

Mr /B54   The Bissell Co. Boyd and Westfall. 391-3.
A test market operation for a new product is planned in three cities.

Mr /B63   Bonham Steel Corp. Boyd and Westfall. 351-2.
A new advertising campaign is pretested on a sample of magazine readers.

Mr /B631 Bonham Steel Corp. Boyd and Westfall. 238-9.
The value of a trademark is analyzed.

Mr /B632 Bookmark Stores, Inc. Lockley and Dirksen.
184-8.
Questionnaires and customer surveys are used with market research done to determine the site location for new branches of a supermarket.

Mr /B633 The Borden Co. Brown, England and Matthews.
il. 732-54.
In order to develop an advertising campaign for an product, the advertising agency conducts a motivational research study to determine consumers' attitudes towards the product.

Mr /B69   Boyington Research Agency. Boyd and Westfall.
455-8.
A research firm conducts research to determine the characteristics of users and potential users of a prepared food product.

Mr /B73   Bramton Co. Bursk (1962). diag. 108-12.
A market research study is done to determine whether a company should enter a new market.

Mr /B89   Esther Burch, Inc. Boyd and Westfall. 239-43.
A toiletry and cosmetic manufacturer analyzes the
choice of models for its advertisements.

Mr /B94   Burns Co. Boyd and Westfall. 141-4.
An automobile battery company proposes to test
the effectiveness of a direct mail advertising
campaign.

Mr /B95   Burton and Co. Lockley and Dirksen. diag.
205-8.
A company determines the nature of the potential
market for its product.

Mr /C17   Carborundum Co. Bursk (1962). diag. 426-32.
Services offered by a company are studied by
interviews in light of industry practice and of
the company's market position.

Mr /C36   A Channel That Created an Industry. Ferber,
Blankertz and Hollander. 492-6.
The organization and responsibility of a market
research department for a new garden magazine
is investigated.

Mr /C361 Channels of Research. Ferber, Blankertz and
Hollander. 55-6.
A manufacturer of school supplies initiates a
market research project to help its customers
merchandise its wares.

Mr /C42   Chemagro Co. Boyd and Westfall. 73-7.
An agricultural chemical producer performs a
concept test for a new insecticide intended for the
consumer market.

Mr /C421 Cheyenne Chemical Co. Stanton. 70-1.
The organization of a chemical company for
marketing research is discussed.

Mr /C46   The Chrysler Corp. Green and Tull. 179-82.
The selection and questioning of consumers to test
the company's gas turbine powered car is discussed.

Mr /C74   Continental Gypsum Co. Stanton. 699-701.

In studying plant capacity, executives of a gypsum company decide to forecast sales.

Mr /C741   A Controlled Experiment.   Ferber, Blankertz and Hollander.   340-3.
A user of a radio rating service decides to evaluate the service's ratings.

Mr /C76   Conley Boughton and Associates.   Boyd and Westfall.   617-20.
An advertising agency conducts research to determine the kind of image men have of a given beer.

Mr /C87   Cross-Classification Tables.   Ferber, Blankertz and Hollander.   404-10.
A department store conducts a customer survey to find out why so many credit accounts are small.

Mr /C97   Cutler and Saddler, Ltd.   Green and Tull.   116-8.
A Canadian razor blade firm requests secondary information from a marketing research firm on the American razor blade market.

Mr /D34   Dean Milk Co.   Boyd and Westfall.   350-1.
A milk company conducts research to better allocate its advertising budget.

Mr /D36   Defense Marketing in the Midwest.   Ferber, Blankertz and Hollander.   diag.   165-9.
A civic group hires a research firm to determine why the Midwest was not obtaining more defense contracts.

Mr /D42   Denny Cola Corp.   Boyd and Westfall.   145-7.
A soda manufacturer proposes to run a market test on a new soda dispenser.

Mr /D46   Designing a Multipurpose Survey.   Ferber, Blankertz and Hollander.   228-31.
Sampling design alternatives are analyzed with regard to bias, cost and efficiency.

Mr /D54   Diary of a Research Project in the Television Set Industry.   Bursk (1962).   diag.   31-44.
A thorough research study investigates the reasons

for major changes in market positions of individual companies in the television industry.

Mr /D75   Dow Chemical Co.   Bursk (1962).   diag. 96-107.
In order to decide whether to increase its capacity for a product, a firm investigates long range trends in the consumption of the product.

Mr /D751 Dow Chemical Co.   Bursk (1962).   il., diag. 198-210.
Before marketing a product obtained as by-product of other processes, the company evaluates a market research study analyzing the product, its distribution, market and prices.

Mr /D79   Drawing the Line.   Ferber, Blankertz and Hollander.   609-10.
A research organization refuses to conduct re-search using a sample which biases the outcome of the study.

Mr /D83   Dromedary Co.   Brown, England and Matthews. 755-63.
Two market measurement services are analyzed with respect to information on the movement of products from grocery stores to consumers.

Mr /D89   The Dummy Talks.   Ferber, Blankertz and Hollander.   343-5.
A beer producer tests the influence of bottle color on taste perception.

Mr /D91   Duncan Motor Co.   Thompson and Dalrymple. diag. 142-6.
A manager of a car dealership studies the market to determine why his firm's market share has de-creased.

Mr /Ed4   Editing Responses.   Ferber, Blankertz and Hollander.   399-402.
A frozen food firm investigates the impact of past quality problems on present sales to consumers.

Mr /Em7   Empty Success.   Ferber, Blankertz and Hollander. 556-7.
A newly introduced beer is tested with regard to

brand name familiarity of consumers.

Mr /F19   Fallon Co.   Boyd and Westfall.   563-5.
A research manager evaluates the effectiveness of
an advertising program.

Mr /F21   Fanta Chemical Co.   Bursk and Greyser.   diag.
112-22.
In order to decide whether to increase the production of its product and plant capacity, studies of
potential demand for a product are made.

Mr /F31   Federal Adding Machine Co.   Green and Tull.   il.
402-3.
The impact of altered distribution channels on
a manufacturer is analyzed from a methodological
orientation.

Mr /F51   First Tobacco Co.   Boyd and Westfall.   620-3.
A research director conducts a motivation research
study on the use of cigarettes.

Mr /F72   Follow-up of a Mail Survey.   Ferber, Blankertz
and Hollander.   diag.   258-63.
The use of a follow-up mail survey is analyzed
with regard to representativeness of present
replies.

Mr /F76   Format of a Report.   Ferber, Blankertz and
Hollander.   447-55.
Sections of a research report on the advantages
and disadvantages of diversification to a company
are discussed.

Mr /F92   Fro-Gold Packing Co.   Boyd and Westfall. 273-7.
An orange juice manufacturer considers purchasing
a syndicated service detailing brand share data.

Mr /F94   Frustrom Research Co.   Boyd and Westfall. 503-4.
Selection criteria and training procedures of a
field survey firm are detailed.

Mr /G16   Garden Equipment, Inc.   Boyd and Westfall. 188-
90.
A lawn equipment manufacturer conducts a study
directed at consumers and retailers to find why a

new product has not met its forecasted sales.

Mr /G22   Gathering Internal Data. Ferber, Blankertz and Hollander. 377-80.
A department store uses credit ledgers to study the origins of branch store patronage.

Mr /G28   General Electric Co. Brown, England and Matthews. diag. 665-83.
A company's consumer surveys are reviewed in light of its marketing objectives.

Mr /G281 General Industries, Inc. (A). Boyd and Westfall. 228-30.
The marketing research manager of a conglomerate decides whether or not to tie all of the divisions more closely under one name.

Mr /G282 General Industries, Inc. (B). Boyd and Westfall. 623-6.
A conglomerate has an image study made.

Mr /G34   A Giant Sights its Market. Ferber, Blankertz and Hollander. 527-30.
A leading steel company undertakes research at improving its image.

Mr /G88   Grimm Candy Co. Boyd and Westfall. 77-81.
A research organization tests how the addition of an animated cartoon character to its advertising affects brand recognition.

Mr /H31   Hawley Farms, Inc. (A). Brown, England and Matthews. diag. 715-9.
The decision of whether a company takes on a new product is based upon results of a consumer survey using questionnaires and product samples.

Mr /H311 Hawley Farms, Inc. (B). Brown, England and Matthews. diag. 720-5.
The results of a consumer survey involving a questionnaire and product sampling are tabulated and analyzed.

Mr /H33   Haywood Co. (A). Boyd and Westfall. 470-3.
A meat packer studies consumer attitudes toward bacon.

Mr /H331 Haywood Co. (B). Boyd and Westfall. 558-60.
A meat packer proposes to determine the attitudes of housewives toward the purchase of prestuffed turkeys.

Mr /H38 Henry Paper Co. Boyd and Westfall. 277-83.
The marketing director of a branded paper product firm is faced with the decision of whether to subscribe to the Neilson Retail Index.

Mr /H55 Hillcrest Products, Inc. Stanton. 698-9.
A glass cleanser manufacturer plans to forecast sales of a new product.

Mr /H56 The Hilton Paint Co. Gentry and Shawyer. 818-20.
The merits of a consumer survey based on interviews and a random sample to analyze buying behavior are studied.

Mr /H71 Holiday House. Bursk (1962). diag. 299-305; Bursk and Greyser. 92-8.
A mail order firm undertakes a market research study to increase its ability to forecast sales and expand demand for its product.

Mr /H81 Household Products Co. Bursk and Greyser. diag. 40-3.
An analysis is made of the research methods of a consumer test done to predict the reaction of consumers to a product and the overall potential of the product.

Mr /In7 Instructions for Interviewers. Ferber, Blankertz and Hollander. 315-20.
Interviewers are trained in interviewing techniques, in correcting bias, and in handling questions.

Mr /In71 Insured Credit. Ferber, Blankertz and Hollander. 582-4.
A retailer attempts to study the extent to which consumers understand one of his offers.

Mr /In8 The Intensive Group Dynamic Approach. Ferber, Blankertz and Hollander. 189-92.

The use of leaderless group discussion to generate hypotheses with regard to chocolate is discussed.

Mr /In81   Internal Investigation.   Ferber, Blankertz and Hollander.   182-6.
Consultants are hired by a university press to determine the cause of its financial loss.

Mr /In82   International Harvester Motor Truck Division. Boyd and Westfall.   225-8.
The cooperative advertising allowance program of International Harvester is analyzed.

Mr /Ir7   Irradiated Food Products.   Bursk and Greyser. diag.   30-3.
In order to judge consumer attitudes towards a new product, a market research study is done using questionnaires.

Mr /Ir71   Irrmanne Advertising Agency.   Boyd and Westfall. 132-4.
An advertising agency tests the impact of disguising the brand name when conducting brand research.

Mr /J59   Joel Whiteman.   Boyd and Westfall.   583-5.
A vice-president questions whether he should make recommendations for action on the basis of research he conducted.

Mr /K67   Klein Co.   Boyd and Westfall.   191-7.
A firm analyzes the relative merits of mail questionnaires and personal interviews as data collection methods.

Mr /L11   La Crosse Marketing Research Agency.   Bursk (1962).   diag. 173-6; Bursk and Greyser. 37-40.
Questionnaires as a method of data collection are analyzed from the point of view of the merits of surveying techniques.

Mr /L32   Larson Foods, Inc. Faville.   34-5.
A market study involving library research, rather than field work, is analyzed.

Mr /L44   Lawson and Worthingham. Boyd and Westfall. 135-8.

A manufacturer of sauces tests the impact of its cooking school promotion on sales.

Mr /L46   Leader Co. Boyd and Westfall. 89-91.
A publishing firm seeks to find ways of increasing the sales of a specialized book.

Mr /L63   Lincoln-Mercury Division. Rewoldt, Scott and Warshaw. il., diag. 232-46.
A marketing research study is undertaken to decide on the brand name and styling of a new product line.

Mr /L78   A Local Market Study. Ferber, Blankertz and Hollander. 160-2.
A trade association devises an exploratory research study of the luggage market.

Mr /L87   J.J. Loomis. Boyd and Westfall. 134-5.
A cooky and cracker manufacturer conducts an experiment to determine the effectiveness of point of purchase material.

Mr /M12   The M.M. McClure Advertising Agency Defines the Role of its Research Department. Weilbacher. 180-98.
A new management team reevaluates the research department of an advertising agency.

Mr /M26   Madison Grant Fiber Pipe. Boyd and Westfall. 186-8.
A fiber pipe manufacturer studies the extent to which plumbing contractors use fiber pipe on farms.

Mr /M29   Malter Co. Boyd and Westfall. 388-90.
A toiletry company conducts research to test the effect of a "deal" offer.

Mr /M34   The Market for a Cemetery. Ferber, Blankertz and Hollander. 313-5.
A research company analyzes whether a funeral home chain should invest in a new cemetery.

Mr /M38   Massey-Scott. Boyd and Westfall. 190-1.
A research director must decide whether to accept

the findings of a research study after being told
of the interviewing bias.

Mr /M41 A Matter of Inches.   Ferber, Blankertz and
Hollander.   345-9.
A paper company tests the impact of a larger
paper towel size on panel members.

Mr /M46 Measuring the Broker's Value.   Ferber, Blankertz
and Hollander.   612-4.
A broker-builder has a study conducted to determine costs of sales management.

Mr /M461 Mediator Needed.   Ferber, Blankertz and Hollander.
647-8.
A department store shoe buyer changes the scope
of research required for his department.

Mr /M58 Michigan Bell Telephone Co.   Rewoldt, Scott and
Warshaw.   135-41.
In order to improve the effectiveness of its long-
distance sales promotion, a telephone company
undertakes an extensive survey involving motivation
research tecniques.

Mr /M83 Morris Research Co.   Boyd and Westfall.   506-11.
The owner of a marketing research firm desires
a report on how to improve the efficiency of the
field force.

Mr /M94 Muri's.   Thompson and Dalrymple.   95-6.
A change in a store's location results in changes
in its image and pricing policy.

Mr /N42 New Element in a Marketing Situation.   Ferber,
Blankertz and Hollander.   312-3.
The impact of hiring minority-group sales clerks
is studied.

Mr /N421 New Era Specialty Paper Co.   Bursk (1962). diag.
124-7; Bursk and Greyser.   27-30.
In considering the manufacture of a new product,
a company does a research study of its potential
market to determine the competitive standing of
the product, its usage and possible advertising
appeals.

Mr /N422 A New Wrinkle in Bottle Capping. Ferber, Blankertz and Hollander. 525-7.
A dairy and bottle cap manufacturer conduct a
joint research study to determine market acceptance
of a new bottle cap.

Mr /N45 Newhouse and Associates. Boyd and Westfall.
453-5.
A shopping center developer proposes to determine
the number of people who knew of the opening of a
new center.

Mr /N81 Northwest Petroleum Co. Boyd and Westfall.
diag. 340-6.
A petroleum company retains a psychologist to
measure advertising effectiveness of a campaign.

Mr /Ob7 Obtaining Data on the Operations of a Laundry.
Ferber, Blankertz and Hollander. 376-7.
A laundry facing declining sales establishes a reporting system to provide adequate information for
management.

Mr /Ob71 Obstructionist Ethics. Ferber, Blankertz and
Hollander. 614-6.
A research client desires the names of people
interviewed in a research study in order to obtain
prospects for his product.

Mr /Oc69 O'Connor and O'Connor, Inc. Boyd and Westfall.
743-8.
A manufacturer of control devices discusses its
method of establishing a market index.

Mr /Oe7 Oerlikon Synchromatic Watch. Green and Tull.
326-30.
Reactions of consumers to a new type of watch
are analyzed based on verbal questionnaires.

Mr /Ol9 Olympic Soap Co. (A). Brown, England and
Matthews. diag. 696-705.
In order to reach its projected sales volume a
company develops a new product. It tests consumer acceptance by using consumer surveys on
brand name, packaging and product characteristics.

Mr /O191 Olympic Soap Co. (B). Brown, England and
Matthews. diag. 706-9.
The development and analysis of a well-planned
sales test is evaluated.

Mr /O192 Olympic Soap Co. (C). Brown, England and
Matthews. 711-4.
In order to promote the sales of its new product,
a company begins a program of forced sampling
using coupons and price deals.

Mr /Om9 On the Right Track. Ferber, Blankertz and
Hollander. 118-20.
A race track decides whether to eliminate a sub-
sidized "race track rail special" upon the basis of
a questionnaire.

Mr /Or2 Organizing and Precoding Questionnaire. Ferber,
Blankertz and Hollander. 402-4.
A bacon packer organizes a questionnaire to cover
problem areas.

Mr /P11 Pacific States Petroleum Co. Thompson and
Dalrymple. diag. 105-11.
A credit analyst tries to revamp a company's
credit approval procedures so as to reflect the
significance of occupation as a factor affecting
payment habits.

Mr /P111 A Panorama of Supermarket Research. Ferber,
Blankertz and Hollander. 47-52.
Market research conducted by five supermarket
chains is contrasted.

Mr /P26 Pasco Co. Faville. 36-8.
A company seeks to determine the present and
future market of its product. Sources of information to analyze the company's market share, new
product possibilities and proprietary items are
studied.

Mr /P73 The Plumas Manufacturing Co. Faville. 54-6.
In an effort to increase its knowledge about its
market, a company establishes files on the operations, products and marketing effort of its competitors.

Mr /P81   Population Characteristics of Metropolitan Chicago, 1955. Boyd and Westfall. 461-70.
An area sampling design is discussed.

Mr /P92   Prior Executive Opinion and Marketing Research Results. Green and Tull. 29-31.
A study analyzing the degree of correctness of marketing executive decision-making is analyzed.

Mr /P93   Pricing a New Line. Ferber, Blankertz and Hollander. 584-6.
A company attempts to devise a demand curve for a new line of cordless industrial tools.

Mr /P94   A Problem in Sales Measurement. Ferber, Blankertz and Hollander. 380-3.
A soft drink company devises an index of consumer sales instead of using A.C. Nielsen's store audit service.

Mr /P941   A Problem of Packaging. Ferber, Blankertz and Hollander. 440-3.
A pharmaceutical corporation analyzes the dispenser segment of its market in terms of profitability, packaging and relationship to its entire product mix.

Mr /P97   Pure Test Farms Dairy. Bursk (1962). diag. 177-9.
Actual questionnaire responses are analyzed for their reflections on product acceptability, pricing, name and necessary research.

Mr /Q4   Quick Milk Co. Boyd and Westfall. 352-3.
A cake mix firm constructs a questionnaire to determine the cause of a loss in its market share.

Mr /R22   Reactions of French Housewives to Dehydrated Soups. Ferber, Blankertz and Hollander. 192-3.
A motivation research study analyzes attitudinal characteristics of buyers of dehydrated soups.

Mr /R24   Recommendations from a Small Survey. Ferber, Blankertz and Hollander. 443-7.
A fertilizer company considers entering the consumer market for fertilizer.

Case Studies in Marketing

Mr/R241   Redefining the Problem.   Ferber, Blankertz and
           Hollander.   644-7.
           A consultant redefines the objective of proposed
           research after discussing the problem with
           management.

M/R25   The Reed Co.   Boyd and Westfall.   667-70.
           A manufacturer of small electrical appliances
           studies methods of evaluating the effectiveness of
           its advertising.

Mr/R26   Regan Brewing Co.   Boyd and Westfall.   81-3.
           A local brewery conducts a taste test of a new
           premium beer.

Mr/R27   Reliable Clock Manufacturing Co.   Boyd and West-
           fall.   128-32.
           A market research director conducts research to
           determine the level of consumer brand awareness
           before and after radio advertising in a market.

Mr/R31   Research for a New Magazine.   Bursk (1962).
           diag.   215-27.
           An extensive research study involving questionnaires
           and interviews is done to determine the commercial
           feasibility of marketing a news magazine.

Mr/R312   Research for a Retailer.   Ferber, Blankertz and
           Hollander.   648-50.
           A marketing consultant advocates reorganizing
           marketing research activities in a department store.

Mr/R313   A Research Menu for a Home Builder.   Ferber,
           Blankertz and Hollander.   52-5.
           A consultant cites specific applications of marketing
           research to the home construction market.

Mr/R314   Research Program for a Radio Station.   Ferber.
           Blankertz and Hollander.   45-7.
           An independent radio station decides to engage the
           services of a market research firm and examines
           the organization's proposal.

Mr/R315   Research on Display.   Ferber, Blankertz and
           Hollander.   560-4.
           A distillery conducts research on its point-of-

purchase advertising to increase its effectiveness.

Mr /R44   Rikarts Advertising Agency.   Boyd and Westfall.
505-6.
A medium-sized advertising agency considers
establishing a field interviewing staff.

Mr /R95   Ryan Lawnmower Co.   Boyd and Westfall.   70-3.
A research study is conducted to determine the
impact of sound on one's perception of quality of
lawnmowers.

Mr /Sa3   Sales Myopia.   Ferber, Blankertz and Hollander.
435-40.
A haberdashery shop uses research to evaluate
its present merchandising strategy.

Mr /Se1   Seaborg Machine Tool Co.   Bursk (1962).   diag.
211-4; Bursk and Greyser.   18-21.
In determining the national and regional potentials
of a product and realigning the company's sales
efforts accordingly, a company analyzes its
market.

Mr /Se11   Seattle Tent and Awning Co.   Boyd and Westfall.
550-8.
A manufacturer of camping and industrial canvas
products wishes to find the impact his company has
in a specific geographical area.

Mr/Se2   Securing Respondent Cooperation.   Ferber,
Blankertz and Hollander.   263-8.
The problem of a marketing research college class
in motivating respondents to fill out mail questionnaires is discussed.

Mr /Se3   Seeking Support.   Ferber, Blankertz and Hollander.
610-2.
Ethical problems relating to the use of a research
firm to demonstrate a need for a service are discussed.

Mr /Se31   Seeking the Vacuum in Distribution Channels.
Ferber, Blankertz and Hollander.   490-2.
An industrial vacuum cleaner producer conducts a
pilot survey on buying behavior of consumers.

Mr /Se4   Selecting a Method of Tabulation.   Ferber,
           Blankertz and Hollander.   410-4.
           Several life-insurance companies study the extent
           to which business life insurance is used.

Mr /Sh4   Shelby Corn Oils Co.   Boyd and Westfall.   138-41.
           A cooking oil manufacturer proposes to test the
           effectiveness of a new package label.

Mr /Sk3   Skin Game.   Ferber, Blankertz and Hollander.
           533-4.
           A manufacturer of a cosmetic conducts a market
           test of the product.

Mr /So8   Southern Pine Co.   Bursk (1962).   diag.   113-23.
           The feasibility of adding a byproduct as new product
           to its existing line is studied in a detailed report.

Mr /Sp1   Spalding Market Research Associates.   Brown,
           England and Matthews.   il., diag.   726-31.
           The sampling plan of a consumer survey designed
           to analyze television viewing habits is studied.

Mr /Sp3   The Sperry and Hutchinson Co.   Brown, England
           and Matthews.   diag.   684-95.
           A report studying the merits of an expanded sales
           program in a new area and the method of analyz-
           ing the sales potential is investigated.

Mr /St1   A. E. Staley Manufacturing Co. Boyd and Westfall.
           50-2.
           A laundry aid manufacturer conducts a study
           evaluating the sales effectiveness of a radio pro-
           gram which it sponsors.

Mr /St11   State Farm Mutual Automobile Insurance Co.
           Hansen.   il., diag.   234-81.
           An extensive market research plan done to maintain
           a company's leadership in the industry includes an
           analysis of a market survey and a broad psycho-
           logical study.

Mr /St3   Steams Chemical Co.   Boyd and Westfall.   230-6.
           Poor sales performance causes a marketing director
           to authorize a pilot survey to study image and com-
           munication problems of a market segment.

Mr /St9   Stuffer Co. Brown, Englan and Matthews. diag.
47-56.
As a result of a carefully analyzed market test,
a company decides to market its product through
supermarkets on a rack jobbing basis.

Mr /St91   Style-Rite Hosiery, Inc. Boyd and Westfall.
560-2.
On the basis of conducted research, a hosiery
manufacturer decides whether he will continue
advertising or conduct further experiments.

Mr /T13   Taking Tea to See. Ferber, Blankertz and
Hollander. 530-2.
A research study concerning the influence of pack-
aging on sales is examined.

Mr /T22   Technology in Libraries. Ferber, Blankertz and
Hollander. 256-8.
A questionnaire, which uses telephone interviews
and which is designed to determine the role of
technology in libraries, is done in a market survey.

Mr /T28   Testing the Validity of a Judgment Sample.
Ferber, Blankertz and Hollander. 233-6.
A magazine decides to identify the extent of bias
in past studies due to sampling design.

Mr /T39   The Thornton Co. Boyd and Westfall. 386-8.
An advertising manager and research director
discuss the problem of sample size determination.

Mr /T41   Three Depth Interviews on Cottage Cheese.
Faville. 4-9.
In depth interviews on consumers' reactions to a
product are analyzed with respect to the use of
the interview to the producer.

Mr /T411   Three Research Problems. Greif. 71-4.
Market research studies done to analyze market
size and behavior are examined.

Mr /T412   Thriftmart and the Los Angeles Grocery Survey.
Thompson and Dalrymple. diag. 97-105.
A survey of food store shoppers questionning

aspects of their shopping behavior results in
recommendations for the store's merchandising
policies.

Mr /T61 Tools for a New Job. Ferber, Blankertz and
Hollander. 638-43.
A company plans to reorganize and to establish
a new marketing research department.

Mr /T68 Transit Radio, Inc. (A). Boyd and Westfall. 393-4.
A firm conducts a study of bus riders to determine
if a new venture is profitable.

Mr /T681 Transit Radio, Inc. (B). Boyd and Westfall.
565-6.
A firm performs a feasibility study for a new
venture.

Mr /Ur2 Urby Paint Co. Boyd and Westfall. 283-5.
A research manager examines secondary data
sources prior to test marketing.

Mr /Us2 Use of Incomplete Sentences. Ferber, Blankertz
and Hollander. 311-2.
The use of projective techniques to study the
central air conditioning market is evaluated.

Mr /Us21 Use of the Consumer Clinic. Ferber, Blankertz
and Hollander. 186-9.
The use of group sessions to study the efficiency
of distribution is analyzed.

Mr /V26 Van Brocklin Co. Boyd and Westfall. 346-9.
A research department constructs a questionnaire
to determine consumer acceptance of a new cosmetic product.

Mr /V62 Very Best James and Jellies Co. Boyd and
Westfall. 338-40.
The sales and advertising managers ask the help
of a research firm in preparing a questionnaire to
determine the retail distribution of a product line.

Mr /V75 Vine Dairy Co. Brown, England and Matthews.
il., diag. 657-61.

The effects of packaging on product differentiation and sales volume are examined.

Mr /W15 Wallace Co. Boyd and Westfall. 83-9.
A research director proposes a study to determine whether consumers could note differences between two competing spray starches in use.

Mr /W55 What Price? Ferber, Blankertz and Hollander. 579-81.
A bowling alley chain plans to diversify into the swimming pool field. A market research firm conducts a study to determine a pricing strategy.

Mr /W552 What Price Hospitality? Ferber, Blankertz and Hollander. 557-60.
A company decides whether or not to retain a plant tour based on studies of brand adherence and brand loyalty.

Mr /W56 The Wheaton Co. Boyd and Westfall. 458-61.
A packer of canned fruit and vegetables desires additional information on users and non-users of his products.

Mr /W73 Winning the Race for Sales. Ferber, Blankertz and Hollander. 487-90.
A wholesale bakery attempts to find the cause of its poor sales performance to a minority group. The research conducted to solve this problem was inconclusive.

Mr /W731 Winter Sales, Inc. Greif. 67-70.
A mail questionnaire sent out with the hope of discovering the reason for a low sales volume is analyzed with respect to its design and sample.

Mr /W732 The Winters Gas Appliance Co. Gentry and Shawyer. 321-2.
The marketing research effort of a firm is evaluated in terms of the cost of consumer 'surveys in relation to the dollar value of the information received.

Mr /W83 Wolff Drug Co. Brown, England and Matthews. diag. 662-4; Bursk and Greyser. 43-5.

In order to distribute advertising funds in an effective manner, the relative importance of sources information on products is analyzed.

Mr /Z7   Zurcher Paper Specialties Co. Boyd and Westfall. 390-1.
A test market study in three cities is planned for a new product.

New Product Planning

N/Ac3   The Ace Radio and Television Co. Lockley and
         Dirksen. 197-9.
         A company, introducing a new product, decides
         on distribution, pricing and marketing strategies.

N/Al2   The Aldridge Products Co. Gentry and Shawyer.
         843-4.
         The introduction of a new product line involves
         questions of product name, test marketing, and
         overall market planning.

N/Al5   The Allgood Drug Company Develops a New
         Athlete's Foot Remedy. Weilbacher. 97-122.
         A drug company directs its laboratory to develop
         an athlete's foot remedy.

N/Am3   American Telephone and Telegraph Co. (A).
         Brown, England and Matthews. il., diag. 79-89.
         A close analysis of the steps involved in producing
         a new product, establishing its image, and market-
         ing it, is discussed.

N/Am31   American Telephone and Telegraph Co. (B).
         Brown, England and Matthews. diag. 90-8.
         The entire question of marketing services, involv-
         ing a company's obligation to offer the service,
         plus the cost and pricing policies of such a service,
         is raised.

N/Am32   American Telephone and Telegraph Co.-Princess
         Telephone. Bursk and Greyser. diag. 21-7.
         Before marketing a new product, a company under-
         takes a two-city test using a sales test and a con-
         sumer survey to determine the product's market-
         ability and price.

N/Am5   AMI, Inc. Boyd, Clewett and Westfall. 11-4.
         In taking on a new product and diversifying the
         product line, a company must devise a completely

new market plan.

N /Ap2   Apex Hardware Co.   Lockley and Dirksen.   176-8.
In taking on a new line, a wholesaler considers
storage and trucking, packaging, advertising, type
of orders to be received and general market.

N /Au61   Aurora Electronics Co.   Stanton.   242-3.
The design of a product and the effect on cost of
additional product features on the final selling
price are discussed.

N /B72   Bradmore-Owens Co.   Brown, England and
Matthews.   il.   120-30.
A proposal to have the sporting goods department
of a department store take on the outboard motor boat
line is studied with regard to merchandising and
marketing programs.

N /B77   Bristol-Meyers.   Buskirk (1961).   80-1.
The advisability of a trade name chosen for a new
drug product is analyzed.

N /C12   California Prune and Apricot Association.   Faville.
84-7.
An agricultural producers' cooperative studies possible byproducts of prunes as a means of increasing the profitable outlets for their distribution.

N /C16   Candygram, Inc.   Westfall and Boyd.   il.   272-8.
In developing a new product, a company considers
the sales program, market potential and consumer
acceptance.

N /C17   Carborundum Co.   Bursk (1962).   506-12.
Two studies dealing with new product planning
analyze the commercial feasibility, characteristics
and applications of the product.

N /C33   Central of Louisiana Life Insurance Co.   Faville.
95-7.
An insurance company explores the possibilities
of extending its coverage to include property along
with life insurance.

N /C73   Commodity Chemical Co.   Bursk and Greyser.   156-65.

A large scale diversification program which develops a new product line brings up the question of marketing strategies for the new products.

N /D54   Dick Rice-Inventor.   Greif.   103-5.
In marketing a new product, thought is given to the concept of marketing myopia and of test markets.

N /D64   Dixie Instruments, Inc.   Bursk (1962).   diag. 523-30;   Bursk (1965).   98-102.
A company evaluates a product to determine whether to produce it and how to market it.

N /D71   Dominion Motors and Controls, Ltd.   Corey. 15-26.
Alternative product specifications for oil well pumping motors are evaluated with regard to preference of selected market segments.

N /D711   Domino Oil Co.   Brown, England and Matthews. diag.   222-34.
A study of distribution policies, pricing and market potential of a product is made before deciding whether it should be added to the company's product line.

N /D75   Dow Chemical Co.   McCarthy.   699-700.
Failure of a new antifreeze product to gain acceptance is studied.   While the product is of high quality, its price is double that of conventional brands.

N /D751   Dow Chemical Co.   Corey.   il. 8-12.
A new chemical solvent is analyzed in terms of price, distribution channels and impact on present market.

N /D752   Dow Chemical Co.   Hansen.   il.   397-404.
The stages involved in introducing a new product are studied.

N /D91   Duncan House.   Hansen.   diag.   382-5.
A mens' toiletries manufacturer conducts a consumer preference test to determine whether a product is to be marketed.

N/Ea7   Eastern Chemical Co. McCarthy. 696-7.
Reasons for the failure of a new chemical product
marketed to consumers and priced higher than
competing products are analyzed.

N/E12   Electra Oleomargarine. Bursk (1962). diag.
420-5.
The use of test marketing to introduce new products
and the best way to utilize buying patterns as
learned from the test marketing are studied.

N/F75   Ford Motor Co., Special Products Division.
Rewoldt, Scott and Warshaw. 226-31.
Several suggestions are proposed for a name of a
new product line.

N/F83   Fox River Tractor Co. Boyd, Clewett and Westfall. 14-7.
A company decides whether to diversify its
product line and establish a marketing program
for the new product.

N/F85   The Franklin Mason Case. Gentry and Shawyer.
342-3.
An inventor considers two proposals for the
purchase of a patent he holds.

N/G28   General Motors Corp. Brown, England and Mat-
thews. il., diag. 206-9.
The introduction of foreign cars, along with the
American efforts to offset their popularity is dis-
cussed. Specific reference is made to General
Motors' attempts with the Oldsmobile F-85.

N/H34   Healthy Co. Westfall and Boyd. diag. 29-35.
To maintain its position in the industry, a company
designs a market plan for its new products.

N/H53   High Point Electric Co. Faville. 283-6.
The planning of a new product is studied beginning
with the original design, market study, pricing
and distribution.

N/H75   Home Products Universal's Handsome Boy Super
Copper Brightener. Weilbacher. 16-31.

The impact of a new product is evaluated through test marketing and panel-member research.

N /H83 How Chemical Co. Lockley and Dirksen. diag. 203-5.
A company introducing a new product is concerned with strategies of price, market channels, promotion and production levels.

N /In5 Inland Steel Co. McCarthy. 692-4.
Efforts to have a company's new product accepted by customers are evaluated.

N /J71 The Jones Co. Lockley and Dirksen. diag. 168-74.
While instructed to order a new product line, a buyer faces the conflict of inventory in an over-bought condition.

N /K53 Kiddie's Kitchen, Inc. Hansen. diag. 340-5.
A new product line is analyzed with respect to market testing via questionnaires, estimated costs and channels of distribution.

N /L64 Line Material Industries. Boyd, Clewett and Westfall. 67-9.
In marketing a new product, a company decides on the brand policy to follow.

N /L66 The Lipto Lighter Manufacturing Co. Greif. 107-11.
The decision to diversify a company's product line entails extensive evaluation of new products.

N /L71 Litetrap Co. Buskirk (1961). 84-6.
The feasibility of marketing a new product is examined.

N /M17 McGregor Co. Stanton. 243-6.
A company organizes itself for new product production through long-range planning and analysis of consumer behavior, industry trends, and new product ideas.

N /M33 The Margeann Chemical Co. Alexander, Cross and Hill. diag. 638-41.

A chemical firm establishes a product plan for a new product.

N /M34   Marlin Firearms Co.   Brown, England and Matthews.   diag.   99–103.
In order to offset the fluctuating demand of its main product, the company introduces another product which has a steady demand.

N /M55   Merrick Laboratories, Inc.   Gentry and Shawyer. 367–70.
The pricing of a new product assumes importance as a determinant in forming its marketing strategy, and as a factor in deciding whether to market the product at all.

N /M58   Midway Electronics Co.   Buskirk (1961).   2–4.
A firm accustomed to marketing military products attempts to market a new product geared to consumers.   Reorganization of its marketing department and of the managerial policies may be necessary.

N /M581   Midway Electronics.   Buskirk (1961).   76–7.
The attributes of a new product design are examined with respect to their effects on product cost, installation ease, and general advisability.

N /M72   Modern Shirt Co.   (A).   McCarthy. 738–41.
An extensive analysis by sampling of the demand for a company's product is made.   The company hopes to distribute a high quality product on a low-margin basis.

N /M721   Modern Shirt Co. (B). McCarthy.   diag. 742–3.
Efforts at determining how many items would be bought at various prices are made to forecast demand.   The study is based on the costs and markup for its product.

N /N11   Nabco, Inc.   Faville.   82–4.
A company initiates a merchandising and promotional plan designed to boost the sales and profits on its new product.

N /N21   The National Foods Co.   Greif.   117–9.

Before adding a new product line aimed at bringing in large profits, a company polls opinions of its staff and chain representatives, wholesalers and retailers.

N /N42   New Products Aluminum Corp.   Greif.   169-71.
A company investigates new markets and possible new products for its main product line.   Problems in entering established markets and in securing effective distribution are raised.

N /Or2   The Ordway Co.   Alexander, Cross and Hill. 648-53.
The advisability of adding a line of electronic parts and supplies to a present line of industrial supplies, equipment and automotive parts is examined.

N /P81   Pop-tent.   Rewoldt, Scott and Warshaw.   27-9.
A new tent product is traced from invention to market.

N /Q4   The Quincy Co.   Lockley and Dirksen.   211-3.
A company introducing a new product decides on its marketing strategy, competition, brand policy and means of distribution.

N /R13   Rainbow Products, Inc.   Bursk and Greyser. diag. 177-84.
A company's new product planning operation is examined from the view of product research and development and organization structure.

N /R21   The Raynell's Co.   Greif.   302-4.
The difficulties in having a new product gain acceptance with industrial and consumer buyers are presented.

N /R24   Red Cedar Shingle Bureau.   Buskirk (1966).   780-2.
A trade association contacts research organizations to study the market for fire-retardant wood shingles.

N /R26   Regulus Clock Co.   (A).   Brown, England and Matthews.   il.   153-8.

The decision to market a new product is analyzed with regard to the nature of the product and its market.

N/R261   Regulus Clock Co. (B). Brown, England and Matthews. il., diag. 159-84.
The questions involved in selecting product models for the year's new product line are discussed and the decisions of the product planning committee are evaluated.

N/R59   The Rockemorgan Company's Development of the Money Collecting Machine. Weilbacher. il. 32-74.
An advertising agency proposes to increase acceptability of a money collecting machine.

N/Sa4   Samco, Inc. Hansen. 345-6.
The marketing strategy for a new product is planned.

N/Sa5   The Sands Co. Boyd and Westfall. 49-50.
A meat specialty company considers entering the market for non-food items in aerosol cans.

N/Sm4   Smile Toothpaste. McCarthy. 100-1.
A new product developed to reverse the profit decline is not received favorably in its market entry.

N/St6   Stork Photos, Inc. Hansen. il. 347-51.
An analysis of sales opportunities and profitability of a new product based on franchise operations is studied.

N/T22   Technique for Selecting New Products. Bursk (1962). il., diag. 531-9.
Techniques to select new products such as probability, weighting, and index numbers for intangible marketing factors and for long and short run profit potential are studied.

N/T43   Tidewater Mills, Inc. Bursk (1962). diag. 513-7; Bursk (1965). 94-8.
In introducing a new product, a company studies the market to determine the product pricing strategy and retail distribution methods. Market

research studies are analyzed for the above factors.

N/T61   Too Good to be Marketable?   Ferber, Blankertz and Hollander.   486-7.
A drug company considers marketing a multi-purpose germicide.

N/T73   Triton Pump Co.   Brown, England and Matthews. diag.   185-92.
Implications of a company's new product on a distributor of that product line are discussed, focusing on a distributor holding an exclusive franchise.

N/V28   Van Eden Solvents Co.   Lockley and Dirksen. 117-9.
In developing a new product line, a company decides between supermarkets and hardware stores as additional channels of distribution.

N/V38   Van Wart Chemicals, Inc.   Hansen.   diag.   404-18.
A mathematical model is developed to determine the feasibility of new products in light of profitability, promotability, extent of market, and degree of difficulty of manufacture.

N/V56   Ventures, Inc.   Hansen.   il., diag.   336-40.
A company tests and studies the costs and properties of a newly patented product to determine whether to purchase exclusive license rights.

N/W27   Washington Supply Co.   Lockley and Dirksen. 208-11.
A company endeavors to maintain its market position and sales on a new product which it reintroduces after recalling it initially for faulty packaging.

N/W33   Watson Heating Equipment Co.   Boyd, Clewett and Westfall.   diag.   65-7.
Before adding a new product to its line, a company investigates its market.

N/W52   Western Gypsum Co.   Buskirk (1961).   78-9.
In planning a new product, product attributes and names are considered.

N/W84   Wonder Foods Company and the New Friendly Girl
         Market Test. Weilbacher. 233-48.
         A new product formulation is evaluated based on a
         test market. Criteria for test market operations
         are also analyzed.

Pricing

Pg /A12   Alford Gifts. Thompson and Dalrymple. diag.
128-34.
A retailer responds to increased rents by raising
the prices of the store's items.

Pg /A15   Allgood Drug Company and Pricing Policy for
Pain-out Analgesic Compound. Weilbacher. 249-65.
A pricing decision for a buffered aspirin is con-
sidered.

Pg /As6   Asphalt Corporation of America. Boyd, Westfall
and Clewett. 179-81.
Faced with a price war within the industry, a
manufacturer reappraises its pricing policy to
meet the competitors.

Pg /Av7   Avon Corporation. Corey. diag. 172-83.
The problem of pricing a new electric speed
drive is discussed. Data on demand, costs and
investments is analyzed in addition to customer
and competitor reactions.

Pg /B16   Bain Soaps, Inc. Boyd, Clewett and Westfall.
175-6.
A company introducing a new product with strong
competition decides to fair trade it.

Pg /B22   Banner Records, Inc. Raymond. 247-8.
An established foreign language record company
is faced with increased competition from new
companies selling records at low prices.

Pg /B44   Benton Rubber Works. Boyd, Clewett and Westfall. il. 181-4.
A decision of what to charge for a newly
developed product based on the costs of a product
and the competition in the industry is analyzed.

Pg /B65   Bosporus. Lockley and Dirksen. 143-4.

A company's break-even point is determined.

Pg/C33   Ceres Manufacturing Co.   Lockley and Dirksen. 144-6.
The problems of a manufacturer involved with re-
ducing a cash discount allowed to wholesalers are
presented.

Pg/C42   Chemco.   Brown, England and Matthews. 629-32.
A company's pricing policies, which established
the same rates for products at its plants regardless of the different costs involved, and which set
the same rates on some items as its competitors,
are studied.

Pg/C72   Columbia Broadcasting Co.   Brown, England and
Matthews.   diag.   104-10.
In an effort to gain a larger sales volume, the
company decides to lower its prices.   An extensive analysis of the effect on the industry of
the price reductions and the implications for the
company is made.

Pg/C76   Container Corporation of America.   Westfall and
Boyd.   diag.   242-8.
In order to have the prices quoted by salesmen
more accurately reflect the company's marketing
objectives, a program is established to revise the
cost estimating system in which salesmen base the
price by estimating each job cost.

Pg/C88   Cryovac Division, W.R. Grace Co.   Westfall and
Boyd.   256-62.
Competition with other companies producing a
similar product and charging lower prices faces
a company with a product of superior quality.

Pg/C89   Cucamonga Co.   Lockley and Dirksen.   159-62.
Faced with competition and rising prices, a company decides to change its pricing policy.   The
strategies presented are a general price rise or
a separate price rise for each marketing zone.

Pg/D381 DeLuxe Record Co., Inc. Hansen.   789-91.
The decision of a company to accept a contract
for a product is analyzed.

Pg/D58   Dillon Electric Co. Stanton. diag. 487-8.
A revised discount schedule is proposed as a
means to control excessive discounting of a fair-
traded product.

Pg/D71   Dominion Motors and Controls. Corey. diag.
190-8.
A quantity discount schedule is introduced in an
attempt to stabilize a mature market. Competitor
and customer reactions to this strategy are un-
favorable.

Pg/D92   E.I. DuPont De Nemours and Co., Inc. Corey.
il., diag. 161-71.
New product pricing and promotion decisions are
analyzed for plastic piping. The higher price
charged for this product must be justified to consumers.

Pg/Ea7   Eastman-Reid Manufacturing Co. Greif. 231-2.
Decisions whether to lower or maintain a product's
price are made on the basis of maintaining margin
profits and industry conditions.

Pg/Er9   Erwin Stamp Co. Lockley and Dirksen. 152-4.
A firm marketing trading stamps faces growing
competition from a recently formed company. The
program which the older company must follow to
meet the competition is studied.

Pg/G28   General Electric Supply Co. Brown, England and
Matthews. diag. 623-8.
Faced with competitive pricing policies and a newly established pricing policy of its own, a company
encounters a decline in sales in one of its major
lines.

Pg/G79   The Grayson Hotel. Lockley and Dirksen. diag.
146-9.
The decision of a hotel to change its dining pricing
policy from one of complete meal price to one on
an à la carte basis is studied with respect to
profit margins, gross sales, and costs.

Pg/H13   Halifax Co. Faville. diag. 294-7.
The decision to purchase job lots of promotional

items for a men's department store and to market them at a low price is debated.

Pg /H16 Haloid Xerox, Inc. Westfall and Boyd. diag. 252-6.
In producing a new expensive line, a company decides whether it should try to market it along with other, less expensive, models.

Pg /H19 The Hancock Co. Alexander, Cross and Hill. 600-3.
A chemical and drug manufacturer reevaluates its pricing policy and practices.

Pg /H21 Happy Hills Concession. McCarthy. diag. 720-1.
The decision to bid on a concession in a recreational park is made based on amount of sales and percent of sales paid to the park.

Pg /H26 The Harvard Crimson. Brown, England and Matthews. diag. 615-22.
A college daily newspaper studies its policies and those of other colleges to determine whether its policies with respect to the sale of national advertising should be altered.

Pg /H31 Hawkins Knitwear, Inc. diag. Bursk and Greyser. 99-103.
A company studies consumer reactions to its decision to change product pricing and packaging policies.

Pg /H55 Hillcrest Products, Inc. Stanton. diag. 484-5.
Pricing a new product involves consideration of its retail price, selling price and the break even point in sales volume and units.

Pg /H551 Hilltop House. Lockley and Dirksen. 287-90.
A newly located resort is concerned with establishing a pricing and advertising policy.

Pg /H83 Howard Frank and Associates. Faville. 305-6.
A manufacturer's agent attempts to regulate the price lines of retailers who carry products of his accounts.

Pg/Im7 Imperial Co. Lockley and Dirksen. diag. 162-7.
The pricing problem involving a firm with several
products facing competition concerns product line
pricing.

Pg/J12 Jack the Barber. Buskirk (1966). 806.
A barber reevaluates his pricing strategy upon the
arrival of a new competitor to his area.

Pg/J15 Jacobson-Rigneur, Inc. McGregor and Chakonas.
diag. 143-6.
A survey utilizing comparison shopping is undertaken to determine the competitiveness of a firm's
pricing practices.

Pg/J35 Jefferson Milk Co. Faville. diag. 306-11.
A company, wanting to decrease the price of its
product so as to increase sales, is faced with
state pricing regulations which set minimum resale
prices.

Pg/J61 John Bache, Inc. Greif. 221-3.
Decisions and methods of establishing a pricing
policy for a new product are discussed.

Pg/K62 Kipling Co. Faville. 278-82.
Questions involving pricing policies of a new
product are analyzed, such as retail price, regional
prices, freight charges and price concessions.

Pg/L14 The Lakeside Golf Club. Thompson and Dalrymple.
diag. 135-7.
A recreational facility debates the merits of offering special group rates to increase utilization of
the facility.

Pg/L45 Lazare Co. Boyd, Clewett and Westfall. 185-6.
Based on product costs, market potential, initial
investment and the general marketing budget, a
company determines the price of a new product.

Pg/L64 Lindel Co. Boyd, Clewett and Westfall. 189-91.
The situation of industrial price competition involving quantity discounts to dealers is presented.

Pg/M25 Macto Co. Hansen. diag. 784-9.

Competitive bidding by a company for a new
product and the analysis of the costs are studied.

Pg/M31   Manhattan Radio Co.   Buskirk (1961).   142-3.
The price level of a new service is discussed.

Pg/M35   Mars Polish Co.   Lockley and Dirksen.   195-7.
In selling to a different market segment, a company faces the decision of changing the price-size
relation of a good.

Pg/M37   Mason Instrument, Inc.   Corey.   diag.   199-213.
Competitive bidding on government contracts is
studied.

Pg/M57   The Metro Manufacturing Co.   Gentry and Shawyer.
398-9.
The decision to sell a large quantity of private
branded products to a mail order house under a
private label is studied.   The manufacturer of the
products maintains that the goods are sold below
cost.

Pg/M61   The Miller Watch Co.   Gentry and Shawyer.   370-1.
A pricing strategy aiming to find the optimum price
for a product examines the theory that consumers
associate the price with the quality of the item.

Pg/M611 Miller, Whitemore and Co.   McGregor and
Chakonas.   150-2.
A pricing policy on job lot merchandise is
discussed.

Pg/M75   Monson Die Casting Co.   Rewoldt, Scott and
Warshaw.   diag.   586-93.
The pricing policy of a company getting business
through competitive bids is studied.   Emphasis is
given to the standard volume concept and cost-plus
pricing.

Pg/N33   G.H. Nelson Co.   Brown, England and Matthews.
il., diag.   602-7.
Faced with increasing competition and steadily
rising prices, the fur department in a specialty
store devises a radically new pricing plan.

Pg /Oa7   Oasis Inn. Faville. 286-9.
A study of a pricing policy of a motel and its proposed rate changes are presented.

Pg /Og5   Oglivie Co. Hansen. 796-8.
The competitive price strategy of one company in
relation to other companies in the industry is
examined.

Pg /Ok4   Oklahoma Oil Co. Westfall and Boyd. diag.
264-9.
A pricing policy for an oil company in newly
taken-over gas stations must consider several
aspects: price cutting, government involvement,
market appeal and brand policy.

Pg /P22   Parker Motor Co. McGregor and Chakonas.
146-50.
Pricing policies of a franchised automobile dealer
are discussed. Emphasis is given to discount and
trade-in practices.

Pg /P76   Polaroid Corp. Brown, England and Matthews.
diag. 608-14.
A company marketing a unique product attempts to
formulate a sound price and discount schedule.

Pg /P81   Pop-Tents. Rewoldt, Scott and Warshaw. diag.
571-9.
The price for a new product to be sold in retail
outlets is determined.

Pg /R31   Resale Price Maintenance: Fact and Fancy. Brown,
England and Matthews. 644-5.
A discussion of the implications of fair trade pro-
visions with regard to resale price maintenance
is held, with emphasis on the role of the Miller-
Tydings and McGuire Acts.

Pg /R54   Robertson, Inc. (A). Rewoldt, Scott and Warshaw.
diag. 593-602.
In distributing its product to competitive distributors,
a company realigns its price structure to maintain
a price differential between distributors and
original equipment manufacturer prices.

Pg /R541 Robertson, Inc. (B). Rewoldt, Scott and Warshaw.
il., diag. 602-8.
A review of competitive pricing practices leads a
company to modify its price policy to wholesale
distributors in its discount schedules and bonus
policies.

Pg /R81 Royal Cushion Co. Faville. diag. 298-305.
A cost analysis is made to study the feasibility
for a company, faced with fluctuating employment,
to market a new product line at the prices
determined.

Pg /Sa7 Sardo Records, Inc. Greif. 209-11.
Distribution pricing decisions are made for a new
product in an unsure market.

Pg /Se5 Seneca Paper Co. Corey. 184-9.
A company's announced price increase is not followed by competitors. Strategies of what action to
take are analyzed.

Pg /Su8 Sure Cut Chain Saw Co. Westfall and Boyd.
270-2.
A new product model entering the market forces
the company to grant discounts to dealers on older
models, resulting in lower profits to the company.

Pg /T17 Tartan Co. Boyd, Clewett and Westfall. 186-9.
A competitive pricing situation in an industry in
which one manufacturer responds to a price increase by another with a drastic reduction in
price is analyzed.

Pg /T22 Technical Products Co. Faville. 282-3.
A company determines the retail price and marketing strategy for its new product.

Pg /T42 Thunderbird Bowling Lanes. Buskirk (1966).
805-6.
A bowling alley proposes a promotional pricing
program for off seasons. It is confronted with
the threat of retaliatory pricing by its competitors.

Pg /T69 The Travel Aide Co. Faville. il. 789-94; Thompson and Dalrymple. 137-42.

A travel agency's plan to market a packaged tour is studied viewing its proposed price in light of the costs of the concomitant promotion and overhead costs of the tour.

Pg/T74 Trolex Sales Co. Rewoldt, Scott and Warshaw. il., diag. 579-85.
Aspects of demand and cost for a new product are considered in establishing its retail price.

Pg/Unt1 Untitled. Converse, Huegy and Mitchell. 688.
A price policy of a wholesale grocer is analyzed.

Pg/V54 Velting Machine Co. Alexander, Cross and Hill. diag. 677-83.
A sales manager recommends that a machine tool manufacturer adopt a policy of leasing machines and selling them.

Pg/V86 Vogue Handbag Co. Lockley and Dirksen. 155-6.
A company manufacturing a high-priced line of goods faces competition and decides whether to lower its prices by producing simpler styles or to retain the same pricing policy.

Pg/W21 Ward Machine Co. Hansen. 791-4.
A trade discount schedule is analyzed.

Pg/W37 Weather Advisors, Inc. Brown, England and Matthews. diag. 595-601.
A service-oriented organization offering specialized weather reports formulates rates based on need for services, benefits to be derived, and ability to pay.

Pg/W52 Western Gypsum Co. Buskirk (1961). 139-40.
The pricing policies of marketing a new product which involve payments of cash rebates are questioned as to legality and ethics.

Pg/W56 Wheatland Co. Stanton. 485-7.
A wholesale jewelry repair service considers changing its pricing policy from a cost basis per item to a single-price system.

Pg/W69 Wiltshire's Department Store. McGregor and Chakonas. diag. 152-60.

Decreases in profits lead a company to study its markdown practices. New procedures are made for price changes.

Pg /W74   Wire Specialties Co.   McCarthy.   719.
A company sets up a consumer products division and studies the marketing strategies and price policy for a new product.

Pg /W78   Witten Corp.   Westfall and Boyd.   262-4.
As a result of a new channel of distribution from hardware wholesalers to retailers, a two price system is adjusted for wholesalers and direct sales.

Pg /W93   The Wright Pen Co.   Raymond.   diag.   270-2.
A company decides the price for a new pen based upon estimated costs, a forecasted demand curve, and psychological considerations.

Pg /W99   Wynn Co.   Hansen.   diag.   783-4.
A company's practice of subcontracting is studied with regard to capacity of the department producing the subcontracted product, product cost, and price.

Pp/Aa1   A and B Chemical Co. Bursk (1962). diag. 458-67.
A company undertakes a survey using interviews to determine the motivations for purchasing its products. The results of the survey are used to analyze the company's advertising policy and improve its competitive position.

Pp/Ab2   Abbott Laboratories. Westfall and Boyd. il. 181-7.
In an effort to elevate a company's image, the company redesigns and repackages its products.

Pp/Ap2   Apex Chemical Co. Bursk (1962). 503-5; Bursk (1965). 91-3.
An analysis of a company entails its product development and research and marketing strategy.

Pp/Au7   Austin Co. Boyd and Westfall. 748-55.
An executive committee is established to make specific recommendations with regard to the future of a division.

Pp/B27   Barrington Co. Faville. 87-8.
A company's decision to produce and promote the sale of a second line of products is studied.

Pp/B31   H.L. Bateman Co. Hansen. 351-3.
An innovation in packaging is introduced and analyzed with respect to its feasibility and profitability.

Pp/B34   The Baylor Department Store. Lockley and Dirksen. 178-81.
A retail, family-operated store increases its merchandise turnover by limiting the number of outlets holding clearance sales and introducing new styles.

Pp/B46   The Best Milling Co.   Boyd, Clewett and Westfall.
          59-60.
          A company diversifies its product with a different
          package style.

Pp/B541   The Bissell Co.   Boyd and Westfall.   713-5.
          A new floor waxer is evaluated by wives of com-
          pany executives and of the company's advertising
          agency employees.

Pp/B63   The Boat Shack.   Thompson and Dalrymple. 91-2.
          The decision to accept an offer of an exclusive
          dealership hinges upon the reliability of the manu-
          facturer and of the product.

Pp/C16   Canadian-Western Paint Co.   Stanton.   246-8.
          Economies in a marketing program, promotion,
          packaging, labeling and general brand policy are
          debated as two companies decide to merge.

Pp/C19   Carlson Lock Co.   Lockley and Dirksen.   192-5.
          A manufacturer of a high quality lock is facing
          competition from those manufacturers producing
          cheaper locks.

Pp/C26   Cascade-Columbia Fruit Growers' Association.
          Stanton.   636-7.
          An agricultural cooperative attempts to differentiate
          its fruit by establishing a brand policy and a pro-
          motional program.

Pp/C35   Champion Sporting Good, Co.   Boyd, Clewett and
          Westfall.   diag.   109-11.
          Trying to improve its sales, a company considers
          diversifying its product line and taking on a related
          line.

Pp/C42   Chemicals, Inc.   Buskirk (1961).   82-3.
          The decision whether to change the formula of a
          product or to design a new product is examined.

Pp/C45   Choisil, Inc.   Hansen.   334-6.
          A company conducts a market research test using
          interviews to determine the company image. Re-
          sults will be used for modifying the product line

Pp/C54　Claremont Candle Co.　Stanton.　240-2.
To reverse a decreasing sales volume, a company
implements its marketing program to appeal to a
different market by adding a lower priced product
to its line.

Pp/C76　Consolidated Packing Co.　Westfall and Boyd.
diag.　178-81.
Faced with private brand competition, a company
decides to modify its policies.　Among possible
choices are lowered prices, a private brand of its
own, or increased advertising prices.

Pp/C761　Continental Appliance Co.　Bursk (1962).　283-94;
Bursk and Greyser.　104-12;　(Bursk (1965).
27-34.
Before introducing a product, a company determines
public acceptability of the product and the market
for the product.

Pp/C762　Conway Clock Co.　Boyd, Clewett and Westfall.
55-8.
A company, selling high quality, fair-traded
merchandise, studies whether to introduce a line
of non-fair traded merchandise.

Pp/D33　Dayton Shirts, Inc.　Raymond.　46-7.
A shirt manufacturer decides the market segment
at which to direct his promotional appeals for his
new product line.

Pp/D35　Decatur Corp.　Corey.　diag.　27-38.
A firm's engineering staff and its distributors dis-
agree as to the design of a new heat pump.

Pp/D351　Decision at Boling Brothers Department Store.
Bursk (1965).　18-9.
A retailer is being convinced by a salesman to take
on his brand.

Pp/D37　Delbar Co.　Buskirk (1961).　73-5.
A firm investigates various products as additions
to its product line.　Also examined are the policies
with regard to new products, investments and
manufacturing activities.

Pp /D75   Dow Chemical Co.   Westfall and Boyd. diag.
           535-43.
           A policy of selling a competitive product through
           private brand markets and in bulk is reappraised
           due to industrial competition, pricing and sales
           forecasts.

Pp /D92   The Duport Co.   Boyd and Westfall.   755-60.
           A soda manufacturer analyzes the market potential
           of each state for his products.

Pp /Es7   The Essex Corp.   Greif.   281-3.
           A sales forecast based on shipping figures is
           studied.

Pp /F26   Fashion Style Clothiers.   Greif.   129-31.
           In planning its strategy for its product, a company
           points to the concept of planned obsolescence and
           marketing segmentation.

Pp /F49   Fine Brew Co.   Boyd and Westfall.   710-3.
           A regional brewery tests the impact of a new
           bottle shape on sales.

Pp /F76   Forest Appliance Co.   Boyd and Westfall. 705-9.
           An appliance manufacturer decides whether an ad-
           ditional feature is worthwhile to consumers.

Pp /F81   Foster Steel Drum Co.   Westfall and Boyd. 157-60.
           A market study is done to determine the potential
           sales of a product to be introduced by a company.

Pp /G29   George Clifford Co.   Faville.   92-4.
           A manufacturer's agent desires to add a compli-
           mentary line to his main product line.

Pp /G291   Georgia Bond Paper Co.   Westfall and Boyd. diag.
           160-3.
           Before manufacturing a new product, a company
           tests the market for the product.

Pp /H11   Hadsell Packing Co.   Lockley and Dirksen. 42-3.
           The sales policies of a company are seen as in-
           adequate with use of private brand and market
           research as suggested improvements.

Pp/H26   Harwick Co. Corey. il., diag. 402-8.
The manufacturer of a new circuit capacitor is told by an end-user that he is unable to utilize this part for nine months. However, the end-user requested that the manufacturer not show the new part to other end-users.

Pp/H81   Household Laundry Products Co. Westfall and Boyd. 175-8.
In adding a new product to its already existing line, a company does a market study for the product, concerning its costs, consumer acceptance, and potential market.

Pp/In8   International Harvester Farm Equipment Group. Boyd and Westfall. 760-7.
A farm equipment manufacturer establishes sales potentials for industrial wheeled tractors in each of its sales districts.

Pp/J31   Jason Supply Co. (A). Corey. diag. 93-104.
A product line audit reveals that several products have substantial net loss. Management is concerned with appropriate action.

Pp/J311   Jason Supply Co. (B). Corey. diag. 105-13.
Based on product line audits, the company evaluates several alternatives of improving product line profitability.

Pp/J62   Johnson Wholesale Drug Co. Lockley and Dirksen. diag. 188-91.
A wholesale drug distributor is faced with the problem of many unprofitable accounts which lower the profits of the firm.

Pp/K33   Kendall Mills. Alexander, Cross and Hill. 629-34.
An interlining manufacturer faces a problem in educating customers about the correct use of its product.

Pp/K63   Kirk Co. Faville. 90-1.
Decisions to add new product lines to a variety store are examined in the light of each department's position within the store.

Pp/L14   Lakeland Dairies, Inc. Hansen. 354-6.
The question of using a private brand ice cream
for distribution in chain stores and/or national
brands in independent outlets is studied.

Pp/L53   The Leland Lock Co. Alexander, Cross and Hill.
635-8.
A quality lock manufacturer must decide whether
to enter the low-priced market because of competitive developments.

Pp/L55   The LePage Co. Greif. 48-50.
A company makes the necessary changes in its
sales policy to introduce a brand name for its
product so as to increase sales.

Pp/L58   Lewis-Shepard Products, Inc. Corey. il. 54-72.
A fork truck company which specializes in manufacturing electric trucks considers whether to add
a gasoline-powered truck to complete its line.

Pp/L62   Liggett Adhesive Corp. Westfall and Boyd. diag.
167-75.
A proposed joint-venture agreement entails the
study of a product's sales potential, sales
organization and competition.

Pp/L621   Lightning Aircraft Co. Bursk (1962). diag.
330-2; Bursk (1965). 35-7.
Aiming to increase its market share, a company
evaluates questionnaires sent to perspective buyers
to determine their product preferences.

Pp/L81   Lockheed Aircraft Corp. Bursk (1962). il.,
diag. 187-97.
A full analysis of the company's sales forecasting methods involving long range planning for
product decisions is presented.

Pp/L97   Luster Co. Boyd, Clewett and Westfall. 58-9.
A company realizes the significance of product
packaging and prepares a test market for its
newly packaged product.

Pp/M19   Mackey Food Stores, Inc. Boyd, Clewett and
Westfall. diag. 60-5.

A supermarket in a chain following a policy of
stocking private brands, as fostered by a cooperative buying organization, decides whether to
change its brand policy.

Pp/M32   Maple Products Cooperative Association. Greif.
113-5.
A cooperative decides on new packaging for its
product.

Pp/M55   The Merry Mart. Lockley and Dirksen. 174-6.
The brand policy of a small independent store
stocking merchandise of only one brand throughout
the store departments is studied. Whether the
store should add a cheaper brand to its shoe line
is debated.

Pp/M58   Microtubes, Inc. Buskirk (1966). 779-80.
A small firm without a direct sales force proposes to enter the defense market for metal tub-
ing.

Pp/M581 Mid-State Manufacturing Co. McCarthy. 686-7.
After researching new applications for a product
and gaining acceptance with the company management, the company tests the reactions of experts
outside of the company.

Pp/M71   Mobil Motors Corp. Greif. 51-3.
A company studies automobile buying motives to
forecast industry trends.

Pp/P21   Park Manor Condominium. Stanton. 161-3.
A retirement community is concerned with its
marketing efforts to attract more people. Market
segmentation looms as an important concept in its
marketing strategy, with especial emphasis on
psychological and sociological factors.

Pp/P22   Parker Printing Co. Westfall and Boyd. 155-7.
A closely related competing product forces a
company to modify its product to meet competition.

Pp/P42   The Perlick Co. McCarthy. 697-9.
Faced with competition in marketing its newly
developed product, a company debates whether to

expand sales of its present line, develop a wider line, or increase sales efforts.

Pp /P61   Pilgrim Co.   Faville.   diag.   71-9.
A company modifies its product policy to meet industry competition.

Pp /P75   Poly Products Co.   Westfall and Boyd. diag. 163-7.
Desiring to expand its product line, a company tests the market for a new item.

Pp /Q2   The Quaker Oats Co.   Boyd and Westfall.   709-10.
A cereal manufacturer decides whether its proposed line of cake mixes has as much consumer acceptance as products of competitors.

Pp /R11   R and S Packing Co.   Greif.   187-9.
The decision of a fruit canning company to use grade labeling is debated.

Pp /R111   Radiation Instrument Co. Corey.   il., diag. 81-92.
A product abandonment decision is evaluated from the perspective of production, sales management and engineering.

Pp /R33   R.J. Reynolds. Buskirk (1961).   diag.   30-2.
Due to strong industrial competition, this firm considers changing its merchandising methods for its main product line.

Pp /Sa3   Sally Crane Casuals.   Faville.   88-90.
A clothing manufacturer is faced with the problem of making profitable use of surplus piece goods.

Pp /Sc6   Scanlon and Co.   Greif.   125-7.
The significance of a product's trademark and brand name is highlighted as a company is brought to court for using a name for its product similar to that of its competitor.

Pp /Sp3   Specialty Products Co.   Boyd, Clewett and Westfall.   53-5.
In trying to offset seasonality of a product line, a company takes on other products in demand at different times.

Pp/T15   R.R. Tank Cars, Inc. McCarthy. 688-9.
The rift between a company's design engineering
department and the sales department is studied.

Pp/T31   Texas Reinforcing Materials, Inc. Faville. diag.
64-71.
A company develops a new product extending its
market to another industry in order to make the
company less dependent on success or failure of
its major product.

Pp/T62   Topic Publishing Co., Inc. Topic Magazine. Bursk
and Greyser. diag. 122-40; Bursk (1962). 141-
55.
A company is concerned for the future prospects of
a product which, although showing profits, is facing difficulties with the company's general policy,
strategy and organization.

Pp/T73   Tritex Chemical Co. Bursk and Greyser. 192-4.
A chemical company must decide on the allocation
of advertising and promotional funds to existing and
new products. The impact of the proposed advertising budget on profitability is examined with
respect to the short and long run.

Pp/Un3   United Air Lines. Westfall and Boyd. diag.
41-9.
In deciding whether to introduce an economy fare,
an airline realizes that qualitative aspects are
significant in industrial competition.

Pp/W32   Watro Co. Corey. il. 39-53.
Faced with design problems, a firm studies
whether to abandon a product even though its
market is increasing at a healthy rate.

Pp/W39   Wedemeyer Electronic Supply Co. Rewoldt,
Scott and Warshaw. 213-7.
Decisions are made by a supply company to add
and delete products from its existing product line.

Pp/W52   Western Mower Co. Westfall and Boyd. 187-90.
A company plans to redesign its package to obtain
lower package costs and eliminate product damage
from faulty packaging.

Pp/W54   Weyerhauser Co. Buskirk (1966). 782-5.
A lumber mill decides whether it should market
a lower grade plywood.

Pp/W67   Williams Co. Lockley and Dirksen. 181-4.
An insurance company debates the problem of
carrying an expensive automobile policy. If it is
dropped, the company would risk losing several
customers.

Pp/W84   The Wonder Foods Company and Market Potential
for Picture Pretty Deluxe Cake Mixes. Weilbacher. 75-93.
Research is conducted to determine whether an
opportunity exists to introduce profitably a new
line of cake mixes.

Pp/W841 Wonder Foods Company Develops a Flanker
Product. Weilbacher. diag. 124-57.
A cake mix company analyzes the market for
instant frosting mixes.

Pp/W842 Wonder Foods Company and New Friendly Girl
Product Development. Weilbacher. 220-32.
A four-pronged study of the chocolate topping
market is made involving motivational research,
concept testing, product testing and test marketing.

Pp/Y2   Yard-Man, Inc. Rewoldt, Scott and Warshaw.
diag. 218-25.
A company considers adding new products to its
existing line or initiating a policy of dual distribution to utilize its excess plant capacity.

Pp/Z1   Zales. Rachman and Elam. 26-8.
Efforts to differentiate products from those of
similar stores are analyzed.

Promotion

Pt /Ab2   Abbott Laboratories.   Westfall and Boyd.   il.
           281-5.
           A promotional plan is designed to increase con-
           sumers' brand awareness.

Pt /Ad9   Advertising Copy--Hit or Miss?   Hansen.   549-53.
           Criteria for a good advertising copy are studied.

Pt /Al3   Algonquin Advertising Agency.   Bursk and
           Greyser.   il., diag.   1-18.
           Analysis of motivational studies is made by an
           advertising agency to determine advertising appeals
           and strategies.

Pt /Al5   Allgood Dairy Co.   Westfall and Boyd.   472-4.
           A firm analyzes the services performed by its ad-
           vertising agency and the compensation of the agency
           for these services.

Pt /Am3   American Dairy Assn.   Boyd, Clewett and West-
           fall.   145-50.
           An advertising program concerned with promoting
           a product through presenting a product image not
           generally held is analyzed.

Pt /Am31   American Telephone and Telegraph Co.   Princess
           Telephone.   Bursk and Greyser.   il.,   diag.
           74-85.
           A market test is undertaken to determine market
           size and the effectiveness of a proposed advertis-
           ing campaign.

Pt /Am32   AMI, Inc.   Boyd, Clewett and Westfall.   141-3.
           An analysis of a complete promotion policy for a
           newly introduced product is conducted.

Pt /An1   Analysis of Soft Drink Spending.   Engel, Wales
           and Warshaw.   571-9.
           The media strategy of the large firms in the soft

drink industry is examined.

Pt /Ar5   Armstrong Appliance Co. Brown, England and
Matthews. diag. 357-69.
Due to a decline in sales, a company decides to
cut its advertising budget.

Pt /Au4   The August Chevrolet Agency. Thompson and
Dalrymple. diag. 157-61.
A car dealer discusses the breakdown of his
advertising budget.

Pt /Au5   Aunt Jemima's Buttermilk Pancake Mix. Westfall
and Boyd. il. 328-33.
A promotional policy for introducing new products
based on free premiums is studied.

Pt /B19   Baldwin Supermarket. Boyd, Clewett and Westfall.
diag. 176-9.
In introducing trading stamps to his supermarket,
the owner realizes that he will have to raise
prices.

Pt /B22   Bank of America. Engel, Wales and Warshaw.
565-71.
The media program of a bank is discussed and
evaluated.

Pt /B26   Barone Steel Co. Buskirk (1961). 156-7.
An advertising program is devised for a company
faced with problems of fluctuating levels of plant
operation. What media to use and the role of
personal selling are discussed.

Pt /B28   Baskin-Robbins 31 Ice Cream Stores. Engel,
Wales and Warshaw. il., diag. 521-31.
The advertising strategy of the ice cream franchisor
is evaluated.

Pt /B34   Bay State Abrasive Products Co. (1). Hansen.
diag. 603-10.
A sketch of a company is drawn, including product
profiles, competitors, pricing, budgets and advertising plans.

Pt /B341 Bay State Abrasive Products Co. (2). Hansen.
610-2.

The analysis of an advertising manager's proposal
for one year's advertising is studied.

Pt /B342   Bay State Abrasive Products Co. (3). Hansen.
612-3.
An advertising and sales manager argue over
their respective budgets.

Pt /B343   Bay State Abrasive Products Co. (4). Hansen. il.
613-9.
The analysis of an actual advertising campaign
copy is presented.

Pt /B344   Bay State Abrasive Products Co. (5). Hansen.
diag. 619-24.
The analysis of inquiry data resulting from an
advertising campaign is studied.

Pt /B345   Bay State Abrasive Products Co. (6). Hansen.
diag. 624-30.
The evaluation of the advertising program of the
company, involving personal interviews and mail
questionnaires is made. Its impact on the product
usage, distribution and competition is studied.

Pt /B346   Bay State Abrasive Co. (7). Hansen. diag. 630-6.
A market study sets forth a number of advertising
tasks and recommends different distribution
policies and product and sales force strategies.

Pt /B347   Bayline School for Girls. Westfall and Boyd.
278-81.
A school, trying to attract more students and
raise its endowment fund, hires a consultant to
develop a promotional policy based on public relations, fund raising and direct mail operations.

Pt /B38   Becker Co. Boyd, Clewett and Westfall. 133-4.
An analysis of an expensive, yet effective, promotional policy designed to increase consumer
awareness of a product, is presented.

Pt /B46   Better Soap Co. Bursk (1962). diag. 403-19;
Bursk (1965). 67-8.
In its effort to gain a competitive position in a
new market, a company studies its product's

image, consumer preferences and buying motives.

Pt /B65   Boston Woven Hose and Rubber Co.   Brown,
England and Matthews.   il. 370-4.
A promotional program using an advertising plan
which stresses brand awareness through its jobber
organization, is reviewed in terms of cost effectiveness for budget preparation.

Pt /B85   Buckner Co. Brown, England and Matthews. 44-6.
Since a ten year policy of advertising in trade
journals showed no direct results, a new advertising manager proposes discontinuing that practice
and relying more on house publication circulation
and salesforce.

Pt /C12   California Prune and Apricot Growers Assn.
Lockley and Dirksen.   273-6.
A company tries to promote its product and en-
lists a market research firm to devise an advertising program.

Pt /C16   Cantwell Packing Co. (A) Bursk (1962). diag.
386-92; Bursk (1965). 70-9.
An advertising budget is reviewed with the company's advertising agency and is discussed with
regard to the campaign strategy, product sales
potential and the worth of a new customer. Use
of premiums to obtain new customers is debated.

Pt /C161   Cantwell Packing Co. (B) Bursk (1962).   393-6.
As a means of obtaining new customers, a company
considers proposals for deals and premiums. Brand
loyalty is discussed in light of the proposals.

Pt /C31   The Cardinal Co.   Faville.   240-5.
An advertising specialty company analyzes its
promotional catalog in light of the nature of the
advertising specialty business.

Pt /C58   Cleveland Industries Inc. (1).   Hansen.   596-8.
A promotional plan and market information system
to appraise the plan are devised.

Pt /C581   Cleveland Industries, Inc. (2). Hansen. 598-601.
A proposed marketing plan consisting of test

markets, distribution, sales plan and advertising strategies is studied.

Pt /C582　Cleveland Industries, Inc. (3). Hansen. 601-3.
A sales test comprised of a study of competitive products, package designs, markets, media, distribution and costs is analyzed and outlined.

Pt /B641　Bourbon Brothers Distilling Company and the Selection of Magazine Lists. Weilbacher. 281-97.
A whiskey manufacturer reevaluates his media selection practices based on product consumption characteristics of magazine readers.

Pt /C67　Colbert's Department Store. McGregor and Chakonas. diag. 165-9.
Planning and coordinating the advertising policies of a company entails formal procedures including advertising request forms.

Pt /C75　Conn-Crest Co. Bursk and Greyser. diag. 85-92.
The adequacy of a company's advertising budget as well as its media program involving space in industrial magazines and in the house organ is evaluated.

Pt /C76　The Contadina Co. Engel, Wales and Warshaw. diag. 585-8.
A tomato sauce manufacturer wishes to design a creative strategy for media other than radio.

Pt /C81　Corning Glass Works. Brown, England and Matthews. diag. 433-42.
A complete analysis of corporate advertising and policies related to it is made.

Pt /C86　Crescent Cosmetic Co. Faville. 234-40.
A number of promotional plans are analyzed in terms of suitability in obtaining dealer cooperation.

Pt /C88　Crown Zellerbach Corp. Faville. 258-9.
Having developed a new product, a company promotes it on the basis of a new brand name.

Pt /C882　Cryovac Division, W.R. Grace and Co. Boyd and Westfall. diag. 285-91.

A company bases its advertising program on educating the industrial buyer on the merits of the product, and attempts to market its product on a consumer level.

Pt /D37   De Laney Co.   Thompson and Dalrymple.   diag. 167-9.
In order to reduce stock and increase sales volume, the buyer explores the possibilities of promoting a new price line.

Pt /D41   Dennis Co.   Boyd, Clewett and Westfall.   diag. 136-40.
A company, facing a possible operating loss, considers cutting the promotional budget.

Pt /D82   Drexel Furniture Co.   Brown, England and Matthews.   il.,   diag. 401-32.
An extensive review of a company's past policies is made in appraising a new advertising plan recommended by the company's agency.

Pt /Ea7   Easy Laundry Appliances Division.   Westfall and Boyd.   diag.   62-71.
A company's promotional efforts designed to increase its product line sales by expanding the industry are studied.

Pt /Ed3   Edgerton Co.   Bursk and Greyser.   il. 62-73.
Consumer testing of advertisements is undertaken to make a selection between two advertisements.

Pt /Ef53   Effluvia House Tests Alternative Programs. Weilbacher.   338-52.
A program of test marketing consisting of reduced price promotion of items with poor sales records is discussed.

Pt /El4   Elizabeth Dairy Co.   Boyd, Clewett and Westfall. 27-9.
An advertising strategy change, designed to attract an untapped market segment, is evaluated by a company.

Pt /Em1   The EMBA Mink Breeders Assn., Inc.   Engel, Wales and Warshaw, il., diag. 619-25.

The strategy of a trade association in stimulating reseller support is analyzed.

Pt /F16   Fairmont Brush Co. Lockley and Dirksen. 266-7.
A company with products in different price lines decides how to increase promotional efforts on the lower priced model.

Pt /F87   Freeman Co. Westfall and Boyd. 474-9.
A company's plans to coordinate its advertising division with its advertising agency are discussed.

Pt /C25   Gayley Co. Lockley and Dirksen. 270-2.
A company diversifies by beginning a housing development. It must, however, devise a sound, yet inexpensive advertising program to attract buyers.

Pt /G28   General Foods Corp. Brown, England and Matthews. diag. 490-510.
A complete analysis of a product promotion campaign is drawn, including campaign meetings, strategy development, product line evaluation, sales efforts, store presentation and campaign evaluation.

Pt /G34   Giantcliff Co. Converse, Huegy and Mitchell. 681-2.
The analysis of promotional efforts for a newly-developed product is made.

Pt /G37   The Gilbert Co. Boyd, Clewett and Westfall. 35-7.
A company attempts to combat seasonality for a product.

Pt /G48   Glendora Co. Faville. 274-7.
Despite promotional and advertising efforts undertaken to boost the sales of a company's product line, one large grocery chain does not purchase the product.

Pt /G76   W.T. Grant Co. (A). Engel, Wales and Warshaw. 531-8.
A well-established retail chain decides to undertake a national promotional program. Decisions

are needed on advertising media, communication message, sales promotion and research.

Pt /G761   W. T. Grant Co. (B). Engel, Wales and Warshaw. il.   588-90.
The means of pretesting a creative strategy are examined.

Pt /H15   Hallicrafters Co.   Brown, England and Matthews. il.   375-84.
A company reappraises its marketing and promotional program to develop a new strategy designed to allow the company to recapture its strong position in the industry.

Pt /H151   Hallmark Greeting Cards.   Westfall and Boyd. il.   306-10.
An advertising program based on magazine space and television is appraised.

Pt /H23   Harold F. Ritchie, Inc.   Rewoldt, Scott and Warshaw.   507-11.
Introducing its new product, Brylcreem, a company develops its promotional mix, plans an advertising program with television and radio, and formulates an advertising budget.

Pt /H36   Helix Co.   Faville.   218-20.
A company's efforts to increase its share of the market by increasing consumer brand awareness is analyzed.

Pt /H53   Highmar Recreation Assn.   Buskirk (1961).   22-4.
The problems in promoting a non-profit, private, recreational facility are presented.

Pt /H55   Hillcrest Products, Inc.   Stanton.   558-9.
Several promotional devices are suggested as introductory offers for a new product.

Pt /H73   Holmes Co.   Westfall and Boyd.   469-72.
Methods of selecting a new advertising agency are examined.

Pt /H75   Home Products Universal Handsome Boy Cleanser. Weilbacher.   201-19.

A cleanser manufacturer conducts a test of alternative levels of advertising support in nine territories.

Pt /H83   Howard Rieter and Associates. Westfall and Boyd. 479-81.
The pricing policies of an advertising agency are evaluated.

Pt /Id1   The Idaho Potato Industry. McCarthy. diag. 714-5.
Idaho potato growers face a problem of maintaining their market position in light of declining use of fresh potatoes and a freight rate disadvantage.

Pt /In2   The Inco "Gleam of Stainless Steel" Promotion. Engel, Wales and Warshaw. 602-14.
The use of promotion funds for in-store dealer support is studied.

Pt /In8   International Harvester Motor Truck Division. Westfall and Boyd. diag. 315-24.
After other industry members discontinue their cooperative advertising program, a company decides whether to maintain its cooperative program.

Pt /In81   International Latex Corp. Bursk (1962). il., diag. 306-12; Bursk (1965). 79-83.
Before investing in extensive television advertisements, this company engages an advertising agency to test the effect of television advertising on the product sales. Another agency is hired to test the influence of television advertising on brand awareness, purchase considerations and product purchases.

Pt /In82   International Minerals and Chemical Corp. Westfall and Boyd. il. 294-301.
A company's promotional program based on providing technical services to the company's customers is analyzed.

Pt /J12   Jack Daniel's: All Goods Worth Price Charged. Engel, Wales and Warshaw. 580-4.
The creative strategy of a premium whiskey is evaluated.

Case Studies in Marketing

Pt /K11 Kaden Manufacturing, Inc. Greif. 245-7.
A company tries to offset shifts in consumer
preferences by more effective advertising and
market research.

Pt /K46 Kerry Kitchens, Inc. Faville. 250-4.
A cafeteria manager tries several promotional
tactics to increase the business of a newly located
branch.

Pt /K83 Koppers Co., Inc. Brown, England and Matthews.
517-23.
Faced with having to plan a sales program in
which distributors and company salesmen are to
devote much time to a company product line, a
district manager studies the distribution and sales
organization.

Pt /L56 Lernaz Department Store. Greif. 237-9.
The use of trading stamps as a promotional device
is discussed from the costs and competitive benefits of using the premium.

Pt /L64 Line Material Industries. Boyd, Clewett and
Westfall. 47-50.
A company develops a contest to promote its
product.

Pt /L88 Lord's Department Store. Westfall and Boyd.
diag. 301-6; Thompson and Dalrymple. 161-7.
Believing that newspaper advertising is inadequate,
an advertising manager plans to advertise by
direct mail campaigns, radio and special promotions.

Pt /L94 Loveland Ski Basin. Buskirk (1961). 158-9.
An advertising campaign is formulated for a ski
basin to enable it to utilize its equipment more
effectively.

Pt /M28 Maine Potato Growers, Inc. Hansen. diag.
539-49.
A program of merchandising and promotion imple-
mented to offset inelastic demand and declining
consumption is analyzed.

Pt /M34   Marks Product Co.   Lockley and Dirksen.   213-6.
Alternative strategies in promoting a product with
little product differentiation are discussed.

Pt /M341 Marlboro.   Engel, Wales and Warshaw.   il.
538-553.
A well-known cigarette faces resistance from
government and industry regulation and from other
filter cigarettes.

Pt /M37   C. H. Masland and Sons.   Brown, England and
Matthews.   diag.   352-6.
A review of a company's promotion and distribution
policies is made in light of its achieving newly set
sales objectives.

Pt /M55   Merrill, Inc.   Rewoldt, Scott and Warshaw.   680-5.
A promotional and advertising program submitted
by an agency to a company entails a consumer
advertising program through magazines, television
and radio, direct mail and point of purchase.

Pt /M58   Michigan State Apple Commission.   Rewoldt, Scott,
and Warshaw.   488-501.
A trade association decides how it can best utilize
an increased assessment in its promotional budget.

Pt /M581 Midwest Precision Corp.   Rewoldt, Scott and
Warshaw.   483-8.
In order to increase its sales volume, a company
considers changing its selling policy to meet its
promotional needs.

Pt /M66   Minute Maid Orange Delight: Consumer and Dealer
Promotions.   Engel, Wales and Warshaw.   il.,
diag.   590-601.
A manufacturer of frozen orange juice evaluates
his past promotions for use in future years.

Pt /M81   Morefiber Wire Rope Co.   McCarthy.   711-12.
A company debates the feasibility of placing a
successful salesman in charge of promoting a new
product and risks the possible decline in sales in
his sales territory.

Pt /M82   Morgan-Oakes Co.   Faville.   228.

Newspaper advertising copy is tested as the main focus of a campaign for a new product.

Pt /M822   Morpurgo Co.   Faville.   3-4.
A company decides to adopt a labeling policy involving either U.S. Government grade labels or a policy of descriptive labeling.

Pt /M86   Mountain States Telephone and Telegraph Co. Buskirk (1961).   164-5.
The methods of promoting the sale of colored telephone sets are presented.

Pt /N17   Nashua Manufacturing Co.   Brown, England and Matthews.   diag.   210-21.
In an effort to change its advertising and brand policies, a company engages J. Walter Thompson to conduct a consumer survey and help the company to develop a new advertising program.

Pt /N18   Nasreldo's Supermarket.   Greif.   241-3.
The adoption by a supermarket of a credit plan serving as a promotional device is discussed.

Pt /N21   National Oil Co.   Buskirk (1961).   166-7.
An advertising strategy including a central product theme, budget and expenditures is analyzed.

Pt /N78   Norman Co.   Faville.   226-7.
In developing a campaign, an advertising agency decides on slogans, appeals and copy.

Pt /N81   Northcott and Associates.   Boyd, Clewett and Westfall.   169-72.
A market research firm investigates the feasibility of hiring a man to increase new business.

Pt /N811   The Northfield Co.   Thompson and Dalrymple. diag.   170-2.
The effectiveness of promoting an imported household item by direct mail and by newspaper is evaluated.

Pt /Ob4   The Oblong Mattress Co.   Converse, Huegy and Mitchell.   678-9.
The problems of producing a product which is

neither nationally advertised nor sold on a price basis are discussed. The possibility of adopting a franchised distribution system is evaluated.

Pt /Oh3   Ohio Tire and Rubber Co.   Stanton.   559-61.
To meet increasing competition, a company decides whether to embark upon a large-scale national advertising campaign or support the advertising efforts of its local franchised retailers.

Pt /Or3   Oregon Feed Research Laboratories.   Faville. 254-8.
The unsuccessful efforts of a company to increase the sales of a new product based on a trained sales force, direct mail advertising and advertising in trade publications are analyzed.

Pt /P11   Pablo Publishing Co.   Faville.   diag.   245-9.
Storebook magazines are analyzed, and one is studied with respect to increasing its circulation and stimulating its advertising lineage sales.

Pt /P19   Pantry Fair Supermarkets.   Rachman and Elam. 104-7.
An advertising strategy for a food chain based on a rotation plan and promotion of specials is analyzed.

Pt /P21   Paris Co.   Brown, England and Matthews.   diag. 455-71.
A department store analyzes a proposal by a trading stamp company that it adopt its stamps. Studies of the department store by the trading stamp company and of the idea of trading stamps by the department store are presented.

Pt /P69   Playskool Manufacturing Co.   Westfall and Boyd. 292-4.
In reviewing advertising expenditures in preparation of the annual budget, an advertising manager reviews the advertising program.

Pt /R11   R and K Sport Shop.   McGregor and Chakonas. 173-6.
Issues in a retail firm's advertising policy concern what to promote, what appeals to stress and how to schedule advertising.

Pt /R15   Ran-Dan, Inc.   Greif.   253-5.
A toy manufacturer attempts to lower costs by
establishing a cooperative advertising program.

Pt /R23   E.J. Reavy.   Lockley and Dirksen.   58-61.
A company's trading stamp policy is analyzed.

Pt /R26   The Regiment.   Buskirk (1961).   162-3.
A men's apparel store devises a promotional plan
to distinguish the store from others in the area.
Such aspects as the role of personal selling and
advertising expenditures are raised.

Pt /R76   Roura Iron Works, Inc.   (A).   Boyd, Clewett
and Westfall.   160-1.
A company's sales and advertising program consisting of small space advertisements and direct
mail is analyzed.

Pt /R761   Roura Iron Works, Inc.   (B).   Boyd, Clewett
and Westfall.   il.   161-3.
A company hires a public relations firm to
analyze its advertising effectiveness and to test
proposed advertising methods.

Pt /R81   Royal Worcester Porcelain Co., Inc.   Engel,
Wales and Warshaw.   il.   614-9.
Royal Worcester's policy of concentrating promotional expenditures at the retail level is
evaluated.

Pt /Sa4   Samson Brewing Co.   Bursk (1965).   84-9.
Faced with a declining market share, a company
undertakes a reappraisal of its selling climate
and marketing activities and plans new advertising
strategies.

Pt /Sa7   SAR.   Rachman and Elam.   21-3.
A promotional program to market educational materials through retail channels is analyzed.

Pt /Sa71   Sarex Watch Co.   Hansen.   diag.   594-6.
An analysis of advertising strategies based upon
television, radio and magazine advertising is made.

Pt /Sc6   Schrafft's Frozen Foods: Achieving Distribution.

Engel, Wales and Warshaw. il. 625-30.
The problems of expanding distribution of a line
of frozen foods into supermarket chains is
evaluated.

Pt /Sc61   Schrafft's Evaluating Newspaper Advertising.
Engel, Wales and Warshaw. il., diag. 639-47.
The application of a method of advertising effective-
ness to a restaurant chain is evaluated.

Pt /Se2   Security National Bank. Buskirk (1966). 807-9.
A new bank establishes a promotional plan.

Pt /Se3   Seeton Packaging Co. Lockley and Dirksen.
279-81.
A food packaging firm wishes to promote its
product by either U.S. Government grade labeling
or descriptive labeling.

Pt /Sh5   The Sheridan Tea Co. Faville. diag. 213-8.
A tea company, hampered by a low advertising
budget, seeks to plan promotional activities. It
also debates whether to join the Tea Council which
advertises the product, regardless of brand.

Pt /Si2   Sigma Instruments. Engel, Wales and Warshaw.
631-9.
An industrial electronic manufacturer plans to
measure the effectiveness of his advertising.

Pt /Si5   Simoniz Corp. Westfall and Boyd. il. 310-5.
An advertising campaign, designed to counteract
implications that a product is no longer essential
is planned.

Pt /Sn5   Snow Mountain Ski Resort, Inc. Greif. 249-51.
The analysis of a proposed resort area for
financial backing and promotional efforts is
studied.

Pt /Sp3   The Speidel Corp. Engel, Wales and Warshaw.
il., diag. 553-64.
Despite the success of an advertising campaign,
management examines the possibility of using
advertising media other than network television.
It is also faced with the problem of building an
adequate dealer inventory.

Pt /Sp8   The Spring Products Co. Gentry and Shawyer.
448-9.
An advertising campaign aimed at particular
markets develops central themes and appeals.

Pt /St2   Standard Finance Corp. Faville. 183-4.
A branch office of a finance corporation attempts
to increase its business. Problems of marketing
intangibles are raised.

Pt /St21   State Camera Co. McCarthy. 691-2.
Plans to sell a particular quantity of merchandise
at a special price do not fulfill expectations.

Pt /St7   Stone Trust and Savings Bank. Boyd, Clewett
and Westfall. diag. 29-33.
A bank develops a promotional plan by studying
its potential market to attract new accounts.

Pt /Su5   Sullivan Engineering Co. Lockley and Dirksen.
138-42.
A company develops a market plan for the sales
of assistance and technical advice to licensees.

Pt /Su7   Sunnyside Furniture Co. McCarthy. diag. 709-10.
The need of a retail sales force to stress socio-
economic preferences of individual groups is
analyzed.

Py /Su71   Sunset Photographic Studios. Stanton. 563-4.
A discussion is presented on promotional devices
needed for new market entry. Whether promotional
programs for new markets must be different from
those in established markets is debated.

Pt /Su72   Surf Motor Co. Westfall and Boyd. 325-7.
A company appraises the merits of participation
in trade shows.

Pt /Sw7   J. Swother's Furniture Co. Rachman and Elam.
108-10.
An advertising strategy based on segmentation of
various markets is employed for a neighborhood
furniture store.

Pt /T23   Television Station Y. Lockley and Dirksen. 291-4.

A television station endeavors to establish a promotional program based on audience ratings.

Pt /T37 Thomson Electric Welder Co. Alexander, Cross and Hill. 675-7.
A resistance-welding machine manufacturer establishes new advertising goals.

Pt /T39 Thornton Co. Faville. 259-65.
An independent appliance distributor, faced with a loss on sales, decides whether to sell to discount houses, increase promotional activities, or leave the business.

Pt /T55 Toastmaster Division. Boyd and Westfall. 670-1.
An advertising agency conducts a copy test of four advertisements to see how they match with the firm's advertising objectives.

Pt /T57 The Tokay Marketing Agreement. Faville. 333-42.
In an effort to increase the demand for their products, growers develop a promotional plan for grapes.

Pt /T65 Towland Corp. Bursk (1962). 322-3; Bursk (1965). 68-70.
A promotional program designed to create demand for a new product is presented. It is based on an introductory demonstration of the product and is followed by successive demonstrations by the distributor in customer plants.

Pt /T89 TvQ. Boyd and Westfall. 269-72.
A cereal manufacturer analyzes a syndicated service for use in planning the advertising budget.

Pt /Un3 The Union Rug Co. Gentry and Shawyer. 447-8.
Media plans concentrating on television and national magazines are analyzed.

Pt /Un31 United States Plywood Corp. Brown, England and Matthews. il., diag. 385-400.
The presentation of an advertising agency's recommended advertising budget and plan is analyzed in light of the company, its products, industry position and past history.

Pt /Unt1   Untitled.   Converse, Huegy and Mitchell. 683-4.
The problems of reaching the market and promoting a specialty product are presented.

Pt /Up8   Upton and Associates. Boyd and Westfall. 665-6.
An advertising agency conducts a copy test to determine the appeal and believability of each of five proposed headlines.

Pt /V24   Valor Ltd. Buskirk (1961). 160-1.
The establishment of an advertising budget including a media schedule is presented.

Pt /V26   Van Loonen Co. Stanton. 561-3.
In order to expand a company's market, its limited promotional program is changed to one involving either a direct mail campaign or a salesman.

Pt /W21   Ward-Knight Furniture Co. Stanton. 488-9.
The use of trading stamps in a new store is initiated as a promotional device.

Pt /W52   Westinghouse Electric Corp. Elevator Division.
Brown, England and Matthews. il., diag. 443-54.
A company, determined to promote a new image of its product, designs magazine advertisements and tests their effectiveness.

Pt /W521 Westinghouse Electric Corp. Elevator Division.
Hansen. il., diag. 553-63.
The study of promotional tests and a proposed advertising campaign through test copies and impact studies is presented.

Pt /W55   The Wham-O Co. Faville. 266-8.
In an effort to increase sales to widen distribution, a company uses jobbers and direct mail, and classified ads and feature articles.

Pt /W59   Whitehall Pharmacal Co. Hansen. 498-501.
A company's dealer promotional policy involving point-of-sale promotion and display discounts is appraised.

Pt /Y3   Yeltown Hardware Co. Lockley and Dirksen.
239-42.

The decision of a retailer who wishes to change the name of his store is studied.

Q/Ar3   Argus. Rachman and Elam. diag. 7-9.
         Methodologies and techniques for measuring price
         differences in food stores are evaluated.

Q/Au7   Austin Co. Westfall and Boyd. diag. 134-41.
         To increase a product's sales potential and
         market share, a company tries to build its ac-
         ceptance and establishes sales goals and quotas.

Q/B41   Bel Air Department Store. Thompson and Dal-
         rymple. diag. 182-4.
         Statistical analyses of departmental operations in
         a retail department store are undertaken, includ-
         ing use of computer programmed multiple re-
         gression equations.

Q/B64   Bordo, Inc. Westfall and Boyd. diag. 117-21.
         A sales forecast for a ten year period is
         analyzed.

Q/B73   Brand A Versus Brand B-A Mathematical
         Approach. Bursk (1962). 23-30.
         A situation involving brand competition is dis-
         cussed, showing how a company can best utilize
         a relative cost advantage in its marketing strategy.

Q/C42   Cherry-Burrell Corp. Westfall and Boyd. diag.
         107-13.
         A company analyzes such items as costs and plant
         capacity to measure its market potential.

Q/C57   Clayton Metal Products Co. Westfall and Boyd.
         diag. 124-7.
         A study of a potential market and future sales is
         made for the marketing plan of a new product.

Q/C76   Consumer Attitudes Toward Irradiated Food
         Products. Bursk (1962). diag. 166-8.
         A study to measure consumer attitudes entails a

survey which is based on a particular sample
design, the adequacies of which are evaluated.

Q/C61   Controls Company of America.   Westfall and
Boyd. diag.   121-4.
A company develops a sales forecast based on
salesmen's estimates.

Q/D92   The Duport Co.   Westfall and Boyd.   diag. 514-7.
A market survey is undertaken to determine areas
for new franchises.

Q/Ed9   Edwards Hardware Store.   Gentry and Shawyer.
289-93.
A mathematical formula is analyzed as an aid
for determining product line profitability and
merchandising decisions.

Q/In8   International Harvester Farm Equipment Department.   Westfall and Boyd.   diag.   99-108.
A company is engaged in research to determine
its product's sales potential.

Q/J31   Jason Supply Co.   Brown, England and Matthews.
diag.   193-201.
A company manager undertakes a study of the
relative profitability of his company's merchandise
lines by determining net profit based on projected
sales and expenses for each product line.

Q/M66   "M. Minty Co.", Hansen.   diag.   50-2.
A company's attempts to arrive at satisfactory
cost estimates and its involvement with competitive bidding are studied.

Q/Or4   Oriole Cigar Co.   Hansen.   diag.   53-6.
Accounting practices of a company for its ad-
ministrative and selling expenses by product
lines are analyzed to lower operating costs.

Q/P71   Pleasant Boots and Stores.   Thompson and
Dalrymple.   diag.   179-82.
Accounting information for a retail store is
studied to yield operating and financial ratios.

Q/Q2   Quantitative Analysis and Education of Future

Executives. Gentry and Shawyer. 529-32.
The use of quantitative analysis by executives
and the role of business schools in training
future executives in these techniques are debated.

Q/R54   Robert Johnston. Rewoldt, Scott and Warshaw.
          141-3.
          Quantitative and qualitative techniques are used
          to determine conditions under which it would be
          economical to purchase an item.

Q/Se4   Selecting Sample Members. Ferber, Blankertz
          and Hollander. 227-8.
          The use of a city directory to generate a random
          sample is discussed.

Q/Se6   Servel Office Supply Co. Westfall and Boyd.
          diag. 127-34.
          An analysis of a sales budget as a planning and
          controlling device is presented.

Q/Sp1   Spalding Market Research. Bursk (1962). diag.
          169-72; Bursk and Greyser. 33-6.
          The adequacy and usefulness of a sample design
          for a survey to determine television viewing
          habits are analyzed.

Q/Sp6   Sportswear, Inc. Greif. diag. 228-9.
          The mathematical calculation of a break even
          point for an enterprise is evaluated.

Q/Sw6   Swiss Lodge. Greif. 310-2.
          A resort owner decides whether to accept a pro-
          posal to lease his lodge or to gamble on weather
          conditions, which if favorable, would yield a
          higher profit.

Q/T66   Toy Transportation Problem. Gentry and
          Shawyer. 493-5.
          The costs of a physical distribution system are
          calculated based on a cost matrix of a shipping
          strategy.

Q/W51   Wessel Starch Co. Westfall and Boyd. diag.
          113-7.

To decide on plant locations, a company
studies consumer market potential for product
usage and regional patterns.

Q/W56   Wheeler Steel Products Co.   Gentry and Shawyer.
293-6.
The analysis of a quantitative model using a
payoff matrix to decide on the best possible
strategy is evaluated.

Q/W75   Wisconsin Door Co. Westfall and Boyd. diag.
141-8.
Trying to deter a falling sales level, a company
has its marketing program analyzed, with long
range plans and sales objectives recommended.

Retailing

R /Al   A to Z Rental Corp.   Rachman and Elam.   diag.
           16-9.
           The decision to secure a franchise involves an
           analysis of the management program of the
           franchisor, its promotional aids and the risks
           involved.

R /Ad41   Adamsville Chamber of Commerce.   McGregor and
           Chakonas.   diag.   9-12.
           From surveys done over a period of years major
           problem areas of retail merchants in a particular
           area are brought to light.

R /Al5   Allen and Barnes.   McGregor and Chakonas.
           diag.   18-22.
           Primary requisites for operating a successful
           retail store and measurement of the degree of
           success are discussed.

R /Al8   Alvin's.   Rachman and Elam.   11-3.
           An evaluation of a specialty store's merchandise
           mix and attitudes towards fashion forecasts is
           made.

R /An1   Andover Merchants Assn.   McGregor and
           Chakonas.   71-7.
           A merchants association investigates the feasibility
           of sponsoring a management training program to
           improve retail management competency.

R /Ar6   Arons.   (A). Rachman and Elam.   diag. 63-5.
           A food chain, faced with a decline in profits,
           analyzes its market share and sales productivity
           in its six strongest marketing areas.

R /Ar61   Arons.   (B).   Rachman and Elam.   diag.   81-5.
           The analysis of a food chain requires examination
           of its merchandising and expense accounts.

R /At9   Atwood, Inc.   Thompson and Dalrymple.   diag.
15-7.
In considering the purchase of an established
clothing retail store, the prospective buyer
evaluates its operating and financial statements.

R /B27   A.A. Barricklow Co.   Boyd, Clewett and Westfall.   diag.   91-4.
A retailer located in a shopping district analyzes
the effects of competition from the stores located
in the new shopping center nearby.

R /B34   Bayside Jewel Shop.   McGregor and Chakonas.
diag.   25-8.
Sound accounting practices for a small retail
store are outlined with prime consideration placed
on their ability to aid in managerial decisions.

R /B51   Bingham's.   McGregor and Chakonas.   diag.
222-4.
The merits of a cash budgeting system and the
establishment of a cash budget for a retail store
are analyzed.

R /B54   Bishop Appliance Store.   Lockley and Dirksen.
90-3.
The role of discount houses in competing with
appliance specialty stores is studied.

R /B67   Bowersox Department Store.   McGregor and
Chakonas.   diag.   123-6.
A retail sales forecasting method is analyzed.

R /B76   Brighton Stores.   Rachman and Elam.   diag.
78-80.
The location of departments within a retail apparel
store is discussed.

R /B85   Buckeye Laundry and Dry Cleaners.   Thompson
and Dalrymple.   diag.   243-53.
A review of a retail store's operations and general
industry trends reveals a decline in sales and
profits.

R /B96   Busy Bee Market.   McGregor and Chakonas. diag.
40-1.

A grocery's margin and profit ratios are analyzed.

R /C13   Callan and Krover. Lockley and Dirksen. 75-9. Several factors, such as site location, finances and business experience are examined before two partners establish a retail furniture store.

R /C24   Carter's Department Store. Thompson and Dalrymple. diag. 227-33. Confronted with excessive markdowns in its shoe department, a department store analyzes its inventory of shoes and the size distributions.

R /C37   Charter House. Buskirk (1966). 786-8. An established men's clothing retailer proposes to introduce a new higher priced line of suits and sport coats.

R /C38   Charles Co. McGregor and Chakonas. 197-200. A store's delivery services are studied in light of a store location.

R /C45   Choosing a Market. Raymond. 86-7. Establishing a retail hardware store raises questions of finance and market segmentation.

R /C61   Clinton Enterprises, Inc. McGregor and Chakonas. diag. 260-6. The problem of receiving approval from a municipality for a neighborhood shopping center is examined.

R /D23   Dans. Rachman and Elam. 75-7. The discussion centers around site location analysis based on traffic counts and their quantitative data.

R /D231   Danta Consumer's Cooperative. Lockley and Dirksen. 95-8. The decision of a consumer cooperative to start another store in a shopping center is analyzed.

R /D28   Davis Super Drugs. Westfall and Boyd. diag. 83-9. A retail drug store considers converting to a self-service operation.

R /D38   Delta Stores. Thompson and Dalrymple. diag.
          202-10.
          An analysis of a department store's inventory
          control policy and procedures is presented.

R /D86   Dudley Camera Shops and Photographic Supply
          Co. Hansen. diag. 73-81.
          The costs of a camera store in its present site
          and in a new shopping center are compared.

R /Ed1   Ed and Jean Kammaran. Greif. 287-90.
          The nature of franchise agreements is described
          as well as are the qualities desired in franchises.

R /F21   The Family Pancake House. Thompson and
          Dalrymple. diag. 271-7.
          A review of the operations of a franchised pan-
          cake restaurant is made.

R /F44   The Fidelity Finance Co. Gentry and Shawyer.
          diag. 92-4.
          A location decision of a finance company is made
          based on the socio-economic market statistics.

R /F66   Floyd Furniture Co. McGregor and Chakonas.
          235-8; Thompson and Dalrymple. 47-52.
          Revisions in a firm's policy to invest solely in
          real estate are suggested.

R /F67   Flynn Supermarket. McGregor and Chakonas.
          diag. 13-7.
          The problem of sales fluctuations in supermarkets
          is discussed.

R /F91   The Friendly Department Store Corp. Converse,
          Huegy and Mitchell. diag. 660-2.
          The decision of whether a large corporation
          oriented towards large department store opera-
          tions should begin discount operations is analyzed.

R /G18   Garnet Co. Thompson and Dalrymple. diag.
          185-8.
          Arguments for and against the leasing of a retail
          department store's television and radio department
          are presented with special stress on the rise of
          service contracts.

R/G35   Gibson's Sewing Machine Co. McGregor and Chakonas. 53-6.
Unable to locate an appropriate site, a company investigates the feasibility of a leased department arrangement.

R/G56   Goldblatt's Department Store. Westfall and Boyd. il., diag. 77-83; Thompson and Dalrymple. 36-43.
A company engages a market research firm to analyze a prospective branch location in a shopping center.

R/G57   Gold's of Nebraska. McCarthy. 703-4.
Factors leading to a customer's displeasure with a department store are suggested, such as store location, credit policy, billing procedure and pricing and premium strategies.

R/G79   Great Lakes Nursery Corp. McCarthy. 695-6.
The profitability of a franchise system is discussed in light of the franchisor's plans.

R/G82   Green Wholesale Grocery Co. Lockley and Dirksen. 93-5.
The role of a voluntary chain in the grocery line is discussed. The nature of the sales force in the chain is also studied.

R/G83   Greene Men's Shop. McGregor and Chakonas. 100-2.
A store owner debates the decision to carry a private label brand of merchandise.

R/H19   Handy Rent-All Center. McGregor and Chakonas. 247-53.
A franchise business is evaluated with regard to benefits, capital requirements, and franchise requirements.

R/H191   Hanover Consumer Cooperative Society, Inc. Thompson and Dalrymple. il., diag. 26-35.
A cooperative's decision to expand the facilities of its grocery store involves analysis of prospective sites and consulting with the cooperative's policy and members.

R /H22   Harmon Equipment Co.   McGregor and Chakonas.
diag. 231-3.
Evaluation of business performance on the basis
of return on capital investment is studied.

R /H23   Harper Brothers Co.   Thompson and Dalrymple.
diag. 237-43.
Problems in retail management and inventory
depletion are discussed in relation to a store's
attempts at conversion to a profitable operation.

R /H24   Harris and Wright.   McGregor and Chakonas.
diag. 37-40.
The use of break even analysis in retail decisions
is evaluated.

R /H241   Harry Smith, Entrepreneur.   McGregor and
Chakonas. diag. 217-22.
An analysis is conducted of initial capital require-
ments confronting a new retail business.

R /H39   Henry Cooper, Druggist.   Converse, Huegy and ·
Mitchell. 655-7.
The merits of a self-service chain drug store are
analyzed.

R /H391   Henry's Tire Service.   McGregor and Chakonas.
diag. 253-7.
Faced with a decline in his profit margin, a retailer decides to make an audit of his competitive
position based on the marketing mix.

R /H55   Hill-Manor Department Store. (A). McGregor and
Chakonas. diag. 113-5.
A system of buying records which facilitates
determination of resources is described.

R /H551   Hill-Manor Department Store. (B). McGregor and
Chakonas. 116-7.
A procedure for evaluating retail suppliers' per-
formance is formulated.

R /H78   Hornaday-Gleason.   McGregor and Chakonas.
233-5; Thompson and Dalrymple. 52-4.
Rental costs of a retail site under various types
of lease arrangements are discussed and compared
to costs of ownership.

R /Ir9   Is the New Branch Store Profitable. Ferber, Blankertz and Hollander. 162-5.
A department store evaluates the profitability of a branch store.

R /J12   L. Jackson and Son Department Store. Lockley and Dirksen. diag. 83-7.
The decision of a retailer to acquire a branch store close to the main store is analyzed based on such factors as profit and loss statements, traffic counts and location.

R /J22   Jamco. Rachman and Elam. 71-4.
The criteria for analyzing retail site locations are evaluated and the responsibilities of market research departments and real estate departments are discussed.

R /J23   James Roberts Dry Good Co. Lockley and Dirksen. 102-4.
The decision to adopt a policy of central buying is analyzed with respect to its effect on buyers and purchasing in general.

R /J33   Jayhawk Clothiers. McGregor and Chakonas. diag. 29-32.
The comparison of the merits of cost or retail accounting methods for a retail clothier is made.

R /J69   The Jones Co. Thompson and Dalrymple. diag. 188-92.
The controller evaluates buyer's purchases against the open-to-buy criteria.

R /J72   Jones Hardware. McGregor and Chakonas. diag. 133-7.
An inventory control system utilizing a unit stock control system is described.

R /K63   Kirk Jewelry Store. Thompson and Dalrymple. 23-5.
A jewelry shop owner must decide whether to move or renew his lease.

R /K77   Knox Building Supply Co. Thompson and Dalrymple. diag. 277-92.

Changes in policy and facilities in a building supply company are planned to adjust to changes in the retail distribution structure.

R/L11   L and A Department Stores, Inc. Greif. 77-9.
Measures which a department store may take to counteract competition of discount operations include passivity, quality improvement and extension of customer service.

R/L73   Littlefield's. McGregor and Chakonas. diag. 210-3.
A study is made of a store's policy on customer returns and of the merits and limitations of a centralized department for returned goods.

R/M35   The Marshall Bass Co. Converse, Huegy and Mitchell. 644-7.
The decision of a company to discontinue its wholesale operations and to establish a retail chain organization is analyzed.

R/M36   Martindale Supermarket. McGregor and Chakonas. diag. 56-8.
Procedures used to evaluate space productivity in retail establishments are established.

R/M45   Marina's Food Markets, Inc. Greif. 93-5.
In order to increase profits and prestige a supermarket chain attempts to establish a gourmet department.

R/M46   Meade Appliance and Furniture Store. Boyd, Clewett and Westfall. 94-7.
A discount house decides whether to expand its product line and move to different locations which have other marketing policies.

R/M53   The Merchants Association of Putnam. Lockley and Dirksen. 67-9.
A town, losing retail business, passes an ordinance prohibiting door-to-door salesmen, as they compete too heavily with the town's retail establishments.

R/M58   The Midway Shopping Market. Thompson and

Dalrymple. 268-71.
A review of the operations of a supermarket is undertaken with changes suggested to reverse the downward profit trend.

R/M581 Milady's Shop. McGregor and Chakonas. 108-10.
Criteria of product selection are applied to a proposed new product line.

R/M84 Morton Hardware. McGregor and Chakonas. 110-2.
In order to decide on alternative product lines, a retailer utilizes a contribution procedure.

R/M97 Musselman's Department Store. Bursk (1962). 384-5.
A department store buyer evolves a new product line by a drug wholesaler.

R/N15 Namms. Rachman and Elam. diag. 66-8.
The characteristics of department store inventory are examined for possible computerization of inventory control systems.

R/N46 Newman Pharmacy. McGregor and Chakonas. diag. 227-30.
Operating and financial ratios for an individual store are compared with industry ratios.

R/N81 North Central Grocery Company Agency Plan. Converse, Huegy and Mitchell. diag. 648-50.
A company analyzes the practicality of establishing two new franchises based on location and operator experience.

R/N811 Northwest Furniture Stores, Inc. McGregor and Chakonas. 46-50.
The formulation and evaluation of an index to be used in site location analysis are studied.

R/P23 Park's Jewelers. McGregor and Chakonas. 204-10.
A comparison is made among various types of credit card plans in relation to retail store credit policies.

R /R15   The Randolf Co. Faville. 27-8.
           In analyzing a department in a large store, plans
           are presented to increase the trade for the
           department and improve its merchandising opera-
           tion.

R /R19   The Rawson Shop. Faville. 23-4.
           A women's specialty store's policy to carry both
           originals and copies of dresses threatens a loss
           of half its clientele.

R /R31   Retail Merchants' Convention. Greif. 85-8.
           A debate centering on the role of trading stamps
           in retail operations as a form of non-price com-
           petition is held.

R /R81   Royal Apparel. Rachman and Elam. 69-70.
           Characteristics of a women's dress shop's in-
           ventory are analyzed in order that an effective
           computerized inventory control system be
           established.

R /R82   Rubicon Co. Faville. 24-7.
           A department store considers changing its opera-
           tion to self-service.

R /R91   Russell-Brown Department Store. Thompson
           and Dalrymple. diag. 112-26.
           A complete analysis of a store's credit policies
           as well as suggestions for improving credit
           management is presented.

R /Sc1   Scrover's. Greif. 81-3.
           The possibility of a full-service appliance retailer
           to maintain a profitable business when faced with
           competition from a discount operation is explored.

R /Se1   Seager Brothers. (A). Hansen. diag. 178-89.
           The development and growth of voluntary groups
           are analyzed in relation to retailers.

R /Se11   Seager Brothers. (B). Hansen. diag. 189-96.
           The analysis of a wholesaler's decision to
           sponsor voluntary groups is studied.

R /Sh1   Shaker Hills Suburban Shopping Plaza. Greif. 89-92.

The factors involved in establishing a hardware store in a new shopping center are examined.

R /Sh11   Shamrock Co. Thompson and Dalrymple. diag. 11-4.
Factors such as site location, product line, supply sources, and expenses are considered when establishing a retail candy store.

R /Sl5   Sloan and Drake. McGregor and Chakonas. 224-7.
Accounting procedures and problems for branch retail stores are presented.

R /Sm6   Smith's Supermarket, Inc. Thompson and Dalrymple. diag. 193-201.
Analysis of the marketing operations of a supermarket is studied to determine how to reduce costs and increase sales volume.

R /So8   Sound or Fury. Ferber, Blankertz and Hollander. 115-8.
A department store attempts to measure the impact of music on store patronage.

R /Sp1   Space Allocation in Dairy Cases of Retail Food Stores. Thompson and Dalrymple. diag. 213-27.
An American Dairy Association study dealing with various methods of utilization of space in dairy cases in supermarkets to maximize sales and gross profits to retailers is presented.

R /Sp6   The Sportswear Mart. (A). Greif. 200-2.
The methods of obtaining inventory value based on a cost method and a retail method are debated.

R /Sp61   The Sportswear Mart. (B). Greif. 203-6.
Operational procedures of a retail apparel store are discussed, such as alteration charges, markdown alternatives, inventory procedures and markdown percentages.

R /St2   State Camera Co. McCarthy. 691-2.
A small business decides to prepare a marketing program and fails. The analysis of this calls for

the study of the store, its market and the
demand for its products.

R /St21   The Status of Retailing. Gentry and Shawyer.
178-9.
The prestige of the retailing industry is analyzed.

R /St4   Stevens Co. Faville. 20-3.
A variety store's decision to stock new items is
analyzed with respect to its merchandising policy
and the position the store holds in its community.

R /St5   G. W. Stiles Co. McGregor and Chakonas.
diag. 130-2.
A store's stock control policy in reordering staple
goods is revised.

R /St9   The Student Union Bookstore. Raymond. 99-100.
A college bookstore manager debates whether or
not to add costume jewelry to his product line.

R /Su7   SuperMarkets, Inc. Hansen. diag. 356-61.
The decision of a supermarket to adopt a private
brand product is analyzed.

R /Sw2   Swank Stores, Inc. Lockley and Dirksen. 72-4.
An analysis is made of a clothing store's policy
to sell merchandise at low prices with a liberal
cash return policy.

R /T73   Tri-State Stores, Inc. McGregor and Chakonas.
diag. 35-7.
A store setting up a cost control system utilizes
cost accounting to allocate indirect expenses.

R /T98   Tyrone Appliance Co. Faville. 29-33.
A store owner considers changing his store policy
as a legitimate appliance dealer to either a partial
discounter or a full-fledged discount house.

R /Un3   University Book Store. McGregor and Chakonas.
diag. 257-9.
Reorganizing a store on a departmental basis calls
for analysis of each department using financial
and operating ratios.

R /Unt1   Untitled. Converse, Huegy and Mitchell. diag.
           687-8.
           The issues of price competition in the grocery
           trade and the factor of trading stamps versus
           supposed lower prices are raised.

R /Unt11   Untitled. Converse, Huegy and Mitchell. 657-8.
           A decision to operate a supermarket based on a
           model involves questions of site location and pric-
           ing.

R /V24   The Valley Construction Materials Co. Lockley
           and Dirksen. 100-1.
           A company's decision to establish a retail opera-
           tion in a new branch store is examined.

R /W17   K.C. Walters Co. Rachman and Elam. diag.
           52-62.
           A variety store chain analyzes a shopping dis-
           trict to determine the usefulness of a site for a
           branch store. Findings of surveys and census
           information are used.

R /W25   Warren Hardware Co. McGregor and Chakonas.
           diag. 50-3.
           The plan to expand a store's operations to an
           additional branch entails a thorough investigation
           of proposed sites.

R /W36   Wayman Department Store. McGregor and
           Chakonas. diag. 126-30.
           A means of stock planning is devised by using a
           merchandise budgetary control policy.

R /W42   Weigand Stores, Inc. McGregor and Chakonas.
           201-4.
           Criteria for judging credit applications are
           discussed.

R /W52   Westgate Department Store. McGregor and
           Chakonas. diag. 103-8.
           A store's merchandising policy with regard to
           preparations for a buying trip are evaluated.

R /W75   Wise Jewelry Store. Thompson and Dalrymple.
           diag. 175-9.

Changes in merchandising policy and promotion
and in relocating the store are suggestions offered to improve the operations of a retail store
faced with lowered profits.

R /Y1   Yancey Pools, Inc.   Thompson and Dalrymple.
18-20.
A franchisee considers dropping his franchise
and taking on the role of an independent business-
man.

Sales Force Management

S/Aa1   A.E.C.P. Co. Faville. 184-7.
A company adopts a sales force compensation
program using an incentive plan.

S/Ad1   Adams-Smith Co. Converse, Huegy and Mitchell.
692-3.
The policies of a company with regard to industrial sales force compensation, expenses and
transference are analyzed.

S/Ag3   Agex Oil Co. (A). Alexander, Cross and Hill.
diag. 556-8.
A company examines its sales organization with
particular regard to its industrial salesmen. It
is felt that the dealer salesmen are provided with
more incentives than are the industrial salesmen.

S/Ag31   Agex Oil Co. (B). Alexander, Cross and Hill.
559-61.
Methods of training the company's industrial
sales force are examined when the company dis-
continues its correspondence course and begins
a full-time course on a division basis.

S/Al4   Alison Pump and Equipment Co. Westfall and
Boyd. diag. 447-58.
Finding a lack of management potential in the
firm's sales personnel, a company evaluates its
compensation program and suggests revisions
based on salary and performance rates.

S/Al5   Allied Business Forms Co. Faville. 179-83.
The question of reciprocity in soliciting business
is raised.

S/Am3   American Hospital Supply Corp. Westfall and
Boyd. 376-83.
The sales divisions of a company, separated by
product type, are analyzed with a view towards

centralizing, decentralizing, or maintaining its present sales force organization.

S/Am32   American Photocopying Equipment Co. Westfall and Boyd. 431-6.
A company reviews its sales programs and studies sales techniques to maintain a line of its business.

S/Ap5   Appliance Distributors, Inc. Bursk and Greyser. il., diag. 46-54.
Reorganization of a company's sales organization to a full-line sales force is studied.

S/B11   B and B Motor Co. McGregor and Chakonas. diag. 77-81.
A franchised automobile dealer works out a sales force compensation plan based on commissions.

S/B18   The Balance Co. Lockley and Dirksen. 233-7.
In trying to raise its sales level to meet quotas for the product, a company reviews its sales force.

S/B48   The Big M Manufacturing Co. Greif. 265-7.
Efforts to increase account profitability are made in amending a company's sales program.

S/B49   Bill Carr. Hansen. 684-7.
The contract agreements between a supplier and a manufacturer are studied.

S/B65   Boston Store. Rachman and Elam. diag. 98-100.
Complaints due to faulty sales coverage in a department store result in an evaluation of part-time help.

S/B76   Bringing up the Rear. Ferber, Blankertz and Hollander. 121-3.
The use of an extensive training program for sales clerks is evaluated.

S/B86   The Buhr Machine Tool Co. Rewoldt, Scott and Warshaw. 358-62.
The use of manufacturer's agents instead of a direct sales force is discussed.

S /B98   The Buyer-Seller Relationship. Gentry and
Shawyer. 419-23.
The respective roles of buyers and sellers and
their status are discussed.

S /C11   Cad Clothing Co. Lockley and Dirksen. 245-7.
A company tries to eliminate the high turnover
in its part-time sales force.

S /C14   El Camino Co. Lockley and Dirksen. 259-62.
A decision to adopt a particular advertising and
sales plan of a company requires the analysis
of the company's sales force.

S /C23   Carran Ceramic Products Co. Greif. 269-71.
The effectiveness of sales meetings in maintaining sales force morale and high sales levels is
discussed.

S /C29   Cases on Retail Selling. Hansen. 670-4.
Four selling situations involving manufacturers
and retailers are examined.

S /C32   R. Cecilia Bakery. Lockley and Dirksen. 250-3.
The training program given to a company's newly
hired employees is analyzed.

S /C54   Clark Auto Sales.   Thompson and Dalrymple.
diag. 67-82.
The sales force of a car dealer is reviewed with
a view towards changing the company compensation
policy.

S /C72   Columbia Furniture Co. Engel, Wales and
Warshaw. 648-9.
Problems in evaluating the effectiveness of furni-
ture salesmen are discussed.

S /D17   Dalton Paint Co. Faville. diag. 187-200.
Various incentive compensation plans for a company's sales force are outlined and evaluated.

S /D52   Dexlo Household Heating Equipment Co. Greif.
262-4.
Steps in the selling process are analyzed in a
training program.

S /D56   Diehl Co. Hansen. 747-51.
Several situations involving the control of the
sales force with respect to demeanor in the selling situation are presented.

S /D75   Dovensher Drug Co. Westfall and Boyd. 403-13.
The situation involving the inadequate performance
of a supervisory member of the sales force is
analyzed.

S /Ea7   The Easterling Co. Westfall and Boyd. diag.
389-95.
The selection, recruiting and training of a company's sales force is studied to reduce a high
turnover rate.

S /Ea72   The Eastville Service Corp. Lockley and Dirksen. 257-9.
A new product marketed by a company does not
readily gain consumer acceptance. The sales
organization, advertising policies, company organization and company history are analyzed in
order to determine the causes and cures.

S /E18   Eltons. Rachman and Elam. 96-7.
The problem of complaints from customers and
the causes of them are discussed.

S /F14   J. M. Fain Co. Converse, Huegy and Mitchell.
669-70.
A company tries to revitalize its old accounts by
planning methods of distributing them.

S /F27   The Faulkner Co. Faville. 174-7.
Due to the inability of a division of the sales
force to meet its sales quotas and to decrease its
high turnover rate, company executives propose
a new method of supervising and training salesmen.

S /F63   Flex Manufacturing Co. Lockley and Dirksen.
268-9.
A company's sales force organization and sales
forecasting methods are studied.

S /F77   Forum Lumber Co. Lockley and Dirksen. diag.
253-6.

In deciding whether to increase the number of the sales force, a company studies the compensation plan, the promotional policies and the ability of the enlarged sales force to gain and maintain accounts.

S/F88   The Freemont Co. Faville. 163-74.
A company's sales force selection policy is re-viewed with special regard to its hiring of trainees. Job applications of future employees are studied.

S/G14   Gambels. Rachman and Elam. 101-3.
In order to provide full sales coverage, a two shift sales system is developed.

S/G29   The George Segal Co. Converse, Huegy and Mitchell. 640-1.
Questions of training company executives are raised when the management of a family-run variety store is taken over by outsiders.

S/G48   Glenn Barnhill. Burskirk (1961). 15-6.
The advantages of a career in selling, over one in technical engineering, are put forth.

S/H36   Hefner Foods, Inc. Westfall and Boyd. 413-7.
With decentralization, a central training school for a company's sales force is closed. The company must establish a new training program.

S/H362   H.J. Heinz Co. Hansen. il. 574-84.
Several sales sketches are illustrated to point out various selling programs.

S/H74   The L.R. Holt Co. Gentry and Shawyer. 417-9.
As an aid in recruiting salesmen with specific characteristics, a sales manager develops a cor-relation test.

S/Im7   Imperial Belting Co. Westfall and Boyd. 395-403.
The high turnover rate of a company's sales force is studied by analyzing the recruiting policies entailing a psychological testing program.

S/In8   International Harvester Motor Truck Division.

Westfall and Boyd. 420-3.
To secure better sales performance a company
appoints a supervisor of training and recruiting.

S/J12   The Jack Wilde Co. Gentry and Shawyer. 471-2.
A company attempts to develop an approach to
forecasting sales volume and to identifying potential customers.

S/J61   John Hancock Mutual Life Insurance Co. Hansen.
700-6.
The selection policy of a firm, involving interviews, personal references, applications and ap-
titude tests is studied.

S/K26   Kehoe, Inc. Hansen. diag. 661-70.
The reorganization of a company from a highly
centralized structure to one which is decentral-
ized in order to benefit the field level sales
force is studied.

S/L21   Lamson Stapling Machines, Inc. Greif. 259-61.
A company's sales organization not defining ter-
ritorial boundaries is examined.

S/L43   Lawrence Foundries, Inc. Brown, England and
Matthews. 559-86.
An extensive review of a company's sales program and that of the industry is made as the
ground work for the decision to reassign sales
force customers on the basis of product
specialization rather than geographical location.

S/L54   Lemay Electric Co. Brown, England and Matthews. diag. 472-89.
The company's sales force organization is traced.
A typical day of a salesman making calls is
described in light of company policies and
objectives.

S/L66   Liquid Chemical Co., Inc. Westfall and Boyd.
diag. 458-66.
A compensation plan is devised to promote the
sales of new, more profitable products.

S/L99   M.D. Lytel Co. Lockley and Dirksen. diag.
221-3.

The basis for the organization of a company's sales force plays a prominent role in the sales of the products.

S/M11   Macomber Specialty Stores, Inc. Greif. 97-9.
A method of sales force compensation in a retail store based on quotas is discussed.

S/M23   McNichols Automobile Sales Co. Boyd, Clewett and Westfall. 144-5.
An automobile dealer devises a selling plan for the sales force designed to better utilize working hours.

S/M27   Magnawatt Co. Bursk and Greyser. 55-8.
Selling and buying strategies are analyzed as factors affecting a company's sales volume.

S/M33   Mariposa Co. Faville. 177-9.
A sales manager must train his sales force to be well equipped to handle problems of customer relations.

S/M34   Marman, Inc. Westfall and Boyd. 502-3.
A company's machine accounting system is studied for application to sales analyses.

S/M37   C.H. Masland and Sons. (A). Brown, England and Matthews. il., diag. 524-41.
The analysis of the use of psychological tests as an aid in sales force selection is presented.

S/M371   C.H. Masland and Sons. (B). Brown, England and Matthews. diag. 541-8.
Steps in formulating sales force compensation and control programs are examined.

S/M75   Monomotors, Inc. Bursk and Greyser. 58-62.
In an effort to increase the sales of its product, a company improves the design of the product and its sales efforts.

S/M85   Motor Car Dealers Assn. Faville. 204-12.
A proposal that salesmen become unionized is considered.

S /M95   A.W. Murphy Co. Lockley and Dirksen. 247-9.
          An automobile dealer studies and tries to change
          its sales force compensation policy.

S /N21   National Thread Co. Westfall and Boyd. diag.
          24-9.
          A sales program is developed to organize the
          sales operations of a company so that the firm
          would have a steady and continuous growth.

S /N36   Nesbit Wire Products Co. Westfall and Boyd.
          467-8.
          The situation involving a policy on bonuses is
          studied.

S /N83   Norwich Publications. Lockley and Dirksen.
          diag. 224-8.
          A company with a loosely structured sales force
          suddenly begins to lose profits with its existing
          sales force.

S /Oc5   O'Connor and O'Connor, Inc. Westfall and Boyd.
          diag. 509-14.
          In order to evaluate the sales performance of
          several branches, a company devises a program
          to determine the relative sales potential of each
          branch territory to act as a standard for com-
          parison with actual sales.

S /Om1   Omaha Paper Box Corp. Brown, England and
          Matthews. diag. 549-53.
          A sales force compensation plan consisting of
          guaranteed salary and expenses on a percentage
          of a salesman's "credit billing" is studied.

S /P29   Payne and Coy. McGregor and Chakonas. 86-90.
          A method is formulated to plan retail sales per-
          sonnel requirements.

S /P43   Personal Selling. McGregor and Chakonas.
          176-82.
          Retail sales presentations are analyzed from the
          point of view of retail salesmanship, responsi-
          bilities to customer and store, and sales
          strategies.

S /R44   Riesen Co. Lockley and Dirksen. diag. 237-9.
A company decides the reason for the decline in
market share is in its sales force, which is then
evaluated by a rating scale.

S /Sc9   Schwartzbrau Brewing Co. Bursk (1962).
518-22; Bursk (1965). 62-5.
To gain a stronger market position for its two
products, each of which require a separate sales
force, a company analyzes its sales force and
product policy.

S /Se6   Series Printing Co., Inc. Westfall and Boyd.
diag. 522-8.
A compensation plan based on a cost estimating
concept designed to encourage salesmen to increase profit rather than volume is studied.

S /Si1   Sims Corp. Hansen. diag. 687-700.
Negotiations and difficulties encountered in a company's efforts to reestablish a large account with
a dissatisfied customer are presented.

S /Sk9   Sky-line Petroleum Co. Faville. diag. 250-4.
A sales supervisor uses brief sketches of personal
histories to illustrate problems in human relations and to serve as bases for group discus-
sions in sales management training sessions.

S /Sp3   Spector Freight Systems, Inc. Westfall and Boyd.
diag. 423-31.
In an attempt to exert greater control over the
sales force, a comprehensive review of a company's sales program is made.

S /St4   Stephen and Kirk. Greif. 273-5.
A sales force compensation policy based on
straight commission is analyzed.

S /St8   Straus Department Stores. Rachman and Elam.
45-7.
A personnel problem involving a buyer and a
divisional merchandise manager is studied with
the possibility of using role playing techniques.

S /Su7   Superior Paper Co. Faville. diag. 157-63.

A proposed plan to reorganize a company's sales force, involving the total merger of the two divisions is evaluated.

S /Su72   Sureness Co.   Westfall and Boyd.   518-22.
Having expanded its operations, a company evaluates the performance of its supervisory personnel.

S /T14   Talcott and Co.   Westfall and Boyd. diag. 439-43.
A study of the product users conducted by the company's own sales force is used to establish sales territories.

S /T39   Thorstad Pipe Co.   Boyd, Clewett and Westfall. 164-6.
A company studies its selling and advertising program to evaluate the need for increasing the sales force activities and the number of salesmen.

S /T61   The Toni Co.   Westfall and Boyd.   417-20.
A company's sales training program utilizing cooperative students on a work-study basis is analyzed.

S /U14   The Ullman Manufacturing Co.   Converse, Huegy and Mitchell.   631-2.
The problems involved in compensating the sales force with expense allowances, client entertainment policies and bonuses are raised.

S /V49   Vebland Co.   Boyd, Clewett and Westfall. 135-6.
A proposal to increase a company's sales force so that the additional personnel would aid the distributors is challenged by the advertising manager.

S /V56   Venture Stores.   Rachman and Elam.   111-3.
A retail store attempts to analyze factors that make a good salesman and to identify those factors in prospective salesmen through tests.

S /V71   The Village Shop.   McGregor and Chakonas.
diag.   90-4.

Fringe benefits, including pension plans for
retail firm employees, are discussed.

S /W15   Walker Products Co. Brown, England and Matthews. 511-6.
The problems of negotiating contracts which have
implications on reciprocal business deals, are
highlighted.

S /W52   Westinghouse Electric Corp. Brown, England
and Matthews. diag. 554-8; Hansen. 742-7.
Evaluating sales performance by means of individual reports and sales performance analysis
records, is studied.

S /W56   Wheeler Tractor Co. Westfall and Boyd. diag.
436-8.
A review of a company's sales costs entails the
study of salesmen's time allocation and general
performance.

S /W64   Wilburton Retailers. McGregor and Chakonas.
183-7.
The status of retail salesmanship and personal
selling is discussed.

S /W67   Williams Department Store. (A). McGregor and
Chakonas. diag. 187-91.
A means of evaluating sales force performance
by isolating specific factors and using letter
grades is described.

S /W761   Williams Department Store. (B). McGregor and
Chakonas. diag. 191-2.
An appraisal of a method of evaluating sales
performance on a quarterly basis is made.

S /W83   Wolff Drug Co. Brown, England and Matthews.
287-9.
A drug company devises a test to judge the influence of its detail men with a view to increasing the number of such personnel.

S /W89   Worcester Co. Hansen. diag. 730-8.
A proposed reorganization of a selling force involving compensation and a control system is
analyzed.

S/Z1   Zales. Rachman and Elam. 24-5.
An effort to offset price competition through
improving selling techniques is studied.

S/Z7   Zenith Co. Converse, Huegy and Mitchell.
684-5.
The implications for a company's selling force
and promotional policies in directing its lines
towards industrial markets are studied.

PART II
SUBJECT INDEX

Building equipment and materials, D/M66, S/D56, S/R44
channel irons, D/C72
competition, R/K77
control joints, Pg/B44
doors, D/P39
gypsum, C/W52, D/W52, I/C76, Mr/C74, Pg/W52
Inland Steel Co., N/In5
lumber, C/P11, S/F77
paper, Mr/N421
pipes, S/T39
plastics, Pp/M581
plywood, Pp/W54, Pt/C88, Pt/Un31
Red Cedar Shingle Bureau, N/R24
shingles, N/R24
steel, N/In5, Pt/V26
storm windows, Q/W75
tiles, D/B271
United States Plywood Corp., Pt/Un31
Burwell Motors Division, Mo/B95
Business education, mathematical structure, Q/Q62
Business forms, S/Al5
Buyer, qualifications, R/St8
Buyer-seller relationship, S/B98
Buying behavior, C/Iv9, C/M58, C/W52, D/D69, I/L49, Mp/K91, Mp/M35, N/C16, R/G56
consumer survey, C/Se5, Mp/K91, Mr/H56, Mr/T412
new product, C/Su7, N/D64, N/R59
product use, C/P11
Buying decisions, research, Mr/M461
Buying influences, price versus quality, Pp/L53
Buying motives, C/C85
automobiles, C/B98
advertising strategy, Pp/A1, Pt/A13 Pt/B46
market entry, C/R15
product pricing policy, Pp/A1

Buying policy, vendor analysis, R/H551
Buying records, resource determination, R/H55
Buying syndicate, D/N82
Buying trips, preparation, R/W52
Byproducts, utilization, Mr/D751, N/M72

Cafeteria
chain location, Pt/K46
promotion, Pt/K46
Cake mixes, Dromedary Co., Mr/D83
California Prune Advisory Board, C/P95
California Prune and Apricot Growers Association, C/P951
Camping equipment, Pg/P81
Candles, product line, Pp/C54
Candy, D/Ob6, L/D38
chocolate, D/C84
retail business, R/Sh11
Candygram, Inc., N/C16
Canning, see Packaging
Capacity, see Plant capacity
Carborundum Co., D/C171-2, N/C17, Mr/C17
Carpeting, D/H67, D/M37, Pt/M37, Pt/Un3, S/M37-1
The Bissell Co., Mo/B54, Mr/B54
flax, Mp/Ar1
C.H. Masland and Sons, D/M37, Pt/M37, S/M37-1
Cars, see Automotive industry
Cemeteries, market for, Mr/M34
Central buying, R/J23
Cereals
National Biscuit Co., D/N21
Quaker Oats Co., Pp/Q2, Pt/Au5
Chain store, drugs, R/H39
Channel conflict, manufacturer and fabricator, D/J36
Channels of distribution, see Distribution channels
Charter House, R/C37
Chemco, Pg/C42

179

Product line expansion (continued)
  profitability, Mp/P53,
    Mr/So8, N/D711, Pp/T73,
    Q/E19 Q/J31, Q/Or4,
    R/M84
    See also Product line
    profitability
  seasonality, N/F83
  tires, batteries and
    accessory products,
    N/D711
  sales and cost allocation,
    Mo/Id2
Product mix, Mp/J77
  department store, R/M97
Product modification, C/D23,
  Pp/C42
  alternative to consumer
    education, Pp/K33
  features, Pp/F76
Product planning, Pp/Aa1-Z1
  See also specific entries
  for individual cases
Product policy, C/D23
Product profitability, improving,
  Pp/J311
Product quality, C/D23, Mp/P94,
  Mp/Un3, Pg/C88, Pg/Ok4,
  Pp/C19
  competitive factor, Mr/B73
  consumer reaction, C/H31
Product usage, C/P19, Q/W51
  demographic correlates,
    N/A15
  threat to market position,
    Pt/Id1
Profit, company organization
  effect, Mo/F11
Profit decline
  new product development,
    N/Sm4
  organizational structure
    relative to, Mo/M58
  relation to markdown,
    Pg/W69
Profit margin, Mr/F21,
  Mr/In8, Pg/Im7, R/B91
  maintenance, Pg/G79
Profit maximization, N/H53
Profit projections, Mg/M46
  new product, Pp/W841

short and long run, N/T22
Promotion, Pt/Ab2-Y3
  See also specific entries for
  individual cases; Advertising
Promotion
  funding methods, Pt/Ef53
  types, Pt/T57
Promotional appeals, determina-
  tion, C/C85
Promotional budget, Pp/W84,
  Pt/M57, Pt/M58
  See also Advertising budget
Promotional efforts, L/B38
Promotional merchandise,
  pricing, Pg/H13
Promotional mix, C/B43, Pp/M
  58, Pt/H22
Promotional program
  failure, Mp/ln2
  objectives, Pt/Se2
  review, Pt/H15, Pt/M37
  sales drive, Pt/G48
Propulsion systems, Mp/K23
Prospects, new product,
  Mp/A18
Prospectus, analysis, Mp/R21
Protective coatings, Pt/K83
Prunes
  California Prune Advisory
    Board, C/P95
  California Prune and Apricot
    Growers Assn., C/P951
  Sunsweet Growers Assn.,
    Pt/A13
Psychological attributes,
  buyers, Mr/R22
Psychological research,
  anxiety reduction, C/Se7
Psychological tests, S/B97,
  S/Im7
  sales force selection, S/M37
Public relations, Mp/H36,
  Pt/B347, Pt/R761
  company performance,
    Mr/W552
  company services, N/Am31
  cost-benefit analysis,
    Mr/W552
  image research, Mr/G34
Publishing, L/D67, Pp/P22
  distribution channels, D/P38

Mr /D64, Mr /T68
random digits table, Q /Se4
sampling frame, Mr /T28,
Q /Se4
sampling universe, Mr /At5,
Mr /N45, Mr /P81, Mr /T39
selecting sample members,
Mr /D46
statistical samples, Mr /B69,
Mr /H33, Mr /N29, Mr /N42,
Mr /P81
telephone sample, N /Sa5
Sara Lee, D /K64
Scheduling, critical path method,
Pp /W841
Schrafft's, Pt /Sc6-1
Scott Paper Co., Mr /M41
Seasonal demand, see Demand
structure
Seasonal fluctuations, see
Demand structure
Secondary data, see Research
data collection
Selective distribution, see
Distribution
Self-service operations, R /D28
changeover, R /R82
Selling, door-to-door, see
Door-to-door selling
Semantic differential, see
Research techniques
Seneca Paper Co., Pg /Se5

Senior citizens, appeals to,
C /Se51
Service club, consumer, Mp /P87
Service operations, R /D28
Service wholesalers, see
Wholesalers
Services
marketing, C /Se2, Mp /B96,
Mp /P87, Mp /R11, N /Am31
pricing, Pg /W37
promoting, Pg /T69
public relations, N /Am31
rental, R /A1
Sheet metal, aluminum, D /K12
Sherman Antitrust Act, L /B63,
L /Sh2, S /W43
distribution, L /J33
Shipping strategy, cost matrix,
Q /T66
Shoe polish, see Polish
Shoes
exercise, N /F85
marketing, Pt /Unt1
retail operations, Q /P71
Shopping centers, Pt /L88,
R /B27, R /D23, R /G56
competitive threat, Mp /R27
economic feasibility, R /C61
location for department
store, R /G56
municipal approval, R /C61
neighborhood, R /C61
rental policy, R /Sh1
site location analysis, R /Sh1
supermarket operations,
R /M58
trading area, Mr /N45,
R /C61
Shopping district, R /B27
branch store location, R /W17
Short run trends, product consumption, Mr /D75
Sigma Instruments, Pt /Si2
Simoniz Corp., Pt /Si5
Site location analysis, R /J22,
R /N46, R /K63
branch store, D /W17,
D /W29-1, Mr /R33, Pg /
J12, R /G56, R /J22,
R /V24, R /W25
cafeteria, Pt /K46

207